SHOOT THAT ONE

MORE ESSAYS BY
JAVIER GRILLO-MARXUACH

"Shoot That One"
More Essays by Javier Grillo-Marxuach

This version first published in paperback, audiobook and ebook in 2019 by Puppet Bureau.

ISBN: 9781794067134

Cover design and Typesetting by Lee Thompson
Cover illustrations by Grant Carmichael
Proofreading and Editorial Assistance by Elizabeth Thurmond

Printed and bound by KDP

www.puppetbureau.com

SHOOT THAT ONE

MORE ESSAYS BY
JAVIER GRILLO-MARXUACH

CONTENTS

INTRODUCTION

by Javier Grillo-Marxuach

Two obsessions fuel the material you are about to read.

One of them is my love of the work of Philip K. Dick. That one is easy to spot, and accounts for the thematic overlap between some of the essays that follow.

Somewhere in my early teenage years, an English teacher gave me the advice that "if you really want to know an author, read everything they have written." I have committed to that deep dive with two authors. The first one is ongoing (Julian Barnes is still alive and producing new work), and the second, Philip K. Dick, resulted in my reading some twenty-eight of his forty-four novels.

Dick's thematic preoccupations - with parallel realities, shifting realities, and realities revealed as false realities designed to mask far worse realities, as well as the plight of characters discovering that their identities have been manufactured for them, or that their identities have been warped by either drugs or aliens, or of characters struggling with and against multiple versions of themselves, of the unreliability of perception and discernment, and the impossibility of knowing the true nature of reality with the gifts we have been given as humans; and his belief that he had been visited by a Vast Active Living Intelligence System in the form of a pink bolt of light that hit him on the head in the early seventies and gave him insight into a possible future - wound up shaping one of the core concepts of my own spiritual being. Dick's constant and deeply paranoid exploration of these ideas ignited in my mind the relatively benign notion that if, in the totality of creation, there can exist an infinite number of possible versions of everything - and of everyone, and of reality itself - then the ultimate expression of all that there is, was, and ever could be, is a state in which all contradictions cease to matter because the totality of existence resolves their conflicts in ways no human could possibly understand.

While Philip K. Dick never suggested (or did he?) that the sum of all being is a superposition of all possibilities in which contradictions no longer matter - something some call God, or god, or Nirvana, or Enlightenment - it is, in my defense, as benign a perversion of his world view as you are likely to find. To believe that every permutation of everything, the good, the evil, and the merely flawed, are part of something much larger - an all-conforming will that gives the whole overwhelming mess that is existence a sort of grand cohesion - feels like a healthy concession to the vastness of the universe, my infinitesimal place in it, and the possibility that there is more to heaven and earth than can be dreamt of in any of my philosophies.

I know. I KNOW. You came here for some juicy backstage gossip about *Lost* and instead I'm giving you some "dog is god spelled backwards" bullshit about how my deep-dive into the work of a mentally ill speed-head sci-fi novelist from the sixties shaped my notions of divinity. Now you're probably wondering how many bong hits you'll have to do just to tolerate the rest of this introduction.

Fine. I'll get to the second obsession fueling the creation of my essays and let you get on to what you really came for.

Ahem. So, yeah: it's a nice thought - limitless

coexistence for limitless expressions of limitless things - but it's not really how the real world works. That is probably why the second obsession I articulate in the majority of this work is what I call "rage for decency": a burning and deeply impatient need for all this shit to just straighten itself up already.

If this strikes you as being at least semi-contradictory with the idea that we are all headed for a place where all is forgiven because all is possible, well, you're at least semi-right. I'm happy to declare that I yearn for something greater, but I make no claim to magnanimity.

In my least magnanimous moments, then, I can't help but see the world as it is today as adolescent. Though I have met many sensitive and thoughtful adolescents, I use the word "adolescent" in the most reductive and pejorative way possible: most days I feel that we have evolved into a society with all the awesome destructive power of adults, and the rash, impulsive, arrogant - and more than occasionally cruel - know-it-all minds of the immature, inexperienced, and unformed. If I had to describe my state of mind in the shadow of Trump's America, the overarching emotion has been: "OH FOR SHIT'S SAKE, GROW UP!"

Of course, one of my rules in the writers rooms of the television shows on which I have worked is that you don't get to criticize anything for which you can't at least pitch a fix. This is why so much of this work tries to articulate not just the anger, but also what I think we could do about the problems at hand. A screed like "The Eleven Laws of Showrunning - The Mean Version" (and yes, the "Nice" - and considerably shorter - one is still available for free on my website) exists not just to berate, but also to offer what I believe to be very commonsensical advice gleaned from some very hard experience. Moreover, in many passages of "The Mean Version" the beratement is the advice, delivered in an alternate form because I have grown so tired of putting it politely and diplomatically throughout the years to no avail. Either way, I do believe that mere venting of the spleen is not only counter-productive, but also just gosh-darned unseemly.

Most days, however, I do wish that a vast, active, living intelligence system would strike me upside the head with a pink lightning bolt, bringing with it a transcendent knowledge of many possible futures, and pasts, and an attendant clarity that would ameliorate the rage with a vision of the unlimited potential of infinity. Of course, insight into a possible future didn't make Philip K. Dick any happier or better adjusted: although it did, apparently, convince him to rush his son to a hospital where a life-threatening condition was quickly, and surprisingly, discovered and resolved in the nick of time. Dick's glimpse into infinity probably did to him what it would do to any of us - it drove him to the verge of insanity by sheer dint of its incomprehensible scope.

Which leads invariably to the flawed individual in the pages that follow. While the totality of truth will forever elude us all - and the work herein reflects a great deal of my frustration with that - I hope that the anger expressed in this collection is illuminating, if not of a higher truth, at least of the mind of someone who lives to entertain, and hopes that in doing so he also leaves behind some ideas worth exploring.

Javier Grillo-Marxuach
Los Angeles, California
November, 2018

KEYNOTE ADDRESS

Fiftieth Anniversary, Creative Writing Program
Carnegie Mellon University
7.15.18

One of my favorite movies is Thomas Alfredson's adaptation of John Le Carré's novel *Tinker Tailor Soldier Spy*. I have seen this film twenty-seven times. I have read the novel twice, along with its sequels. I have also seen the 1976 BBC miniseries and the follow-up *Smiley's People,* both starring Alec Guinness.

To this day, however, I really can't tell you what happens in *Tinker Tailor Soldier Spy...* other than it has something to do with men so profoundly closeted that they <u>just</u> have to destroy the Soviet Union.

That much said, there is one moment that sticks with me in spite of my complete inability to understand the film on the level of plot or character... or really anything not having to do with ugly men's suits from the 1970s. In the scene, Spy Master George Smiley - played here by Gary Oldman - has a painful reckoning with the lifelong friend and colleague he has uncovered as a Russian mole in the upper echelons of British Intelligence.

When asked why he betrayed Queen and Country, the mole replies - with the quivering upper lip of a man who has never, ever, not once, talked about his feelings - that:"It was an aesthetic choice as much as a moral one, and the West has become... so very ugly."

If you think that there is a cheap analogy to be made between that line of dialogue and our current political situation, then let me assure you, you hired the right TV writer for the job.

Like so many sensitive and artistic people who were prone to melancholy even before our democracy went to shit, I feel that the present tyranny is not merely political, but also rhetorical and spiritual. It is a living expression of the belief that the only victories that have value are the ones earned by the fist or the crotch.

Part of where we find ourselves in our politics, discourse, and relationships is the result of a systemic failure of kindness and empathy in our daily practice of living. It is a failure exacerbated by the pernicious yet seductive fantasy that those who act like the rich and cruel will magically gain wealth, and the concomitant entitlement to further, more ambitious cruelty. Too many have bought into the idea that destroying those whose existence annoys us on principle is equal to "winning."

So. What does this incredible bummer have to do with the anniversary of a creative writing program?

Well, I am a writer and, increasingly, an artist... which is embarrassing, because, when I went into TV in the 90s, the medium was straight-up disreputable and I was honestly trying to sell out. Also, I work for other writers in an industry that not only tolerates, but often lionizes a great deal of madness, rage, and abuse in its upper management. I work in an industry that deliberately keeps its barriers to entry stocked with cauldrons of boiling oil, especially for women and minorities. I work in an industry that forces people to move to Los Angeles.

A few years ago, me and a man named Jose Molina - who is not only a dear old friend but also a very accomplished television writer/producer - were sitting at a bar on Ventura Boulevard getting drunk before our weekly *Dungeons & Dragons* game... like you do. As we ordered our second round, we began to list all of the sociopathic abusers for whom we had worked over the years. The resulting list, which could charitably be called "a real cavalcade of sigmoid orifices," was lengthy, and encompassed the majority of both our careers.

As the third round arrived, we fantasized about what it would take to change the character of so many awful bosses to whom we had given our best and most creative work. What kind of Ebenezer Scrooge experience would it take to shift the minds of so many who felt entitled to cruelty, or availed themselves to it through sheer ignorance, to the real work of uplifting their employees instead of torturing them?

Soon however, we came to the depressing realization that, once someone achieves a position of power, it is as if society has given them a validation that their methods do not need to change. A TV network gave you hundreds of millions of dollars to make a show you created. Surely that means you are a genius and beyond correction. So we came up with the idea of making a podcast to, ostensibly, teach newcomers about the TV business. This was an attractive hook, since information about how to break into TV, and how to behave once you're in, is notoriously hard to come by and expensive and seldom accurate when it is.

But that really was just a Trojan Horse for the far more insidious message that you do not have to be an asshole to be successful, an abuser to get your collaborators to perform, or need to destroy everyone out of fear that they will someday come back to murder you and take your place... or worse, tell other people what you were like before you were a Genius.

The podcast has the colossally stupid name "Children of Tendu," it's free, and the twenty or so episodes we have produced to this day have been downloaded over 400,000 times. Based on that, we approached the Writers Guild and spent a year teaching a series called "Living in the Middle" which was intended as a sort of continuing education for writer/producers but really was a crypto-altruistic mental inception made in the name of decency, integrity, and collaboration.

If you know the entertainment business - or try to enter it - then you probably know that a lot of people with far less experience than I will gladly charge you a lot of money for far less and pretend they are giving you the keys to the kingdom. We took forty combined years of hard-earned knowledge and experience and gave it away for free.

The effect this has had on me as a writer, a manager of creative people, and a human being has been immeasurable. I believe in evolution, and evolution means that if your competition is loud, obnoxious, and seemingly victorious, and you are quiet, introverted, and don't have a good publicist, you can still prevail by surrounding the bad guys with people who just plain disagree with them. Evolution is a numbers game, and we each have the power to help make more of us than there are of them.

The efforts I have just described are a tiny little spearhead in that evolution. We arm our audience with knowledge, but also tell them unequivocally that much of what is understood as ordinary behavior in our business is wrong, and if they can't change it, they'd better not feel entitled to further the cycle of abuse with their own actions. If Jose and I wind up helping one person succeed as a television writer while keeping them from falling for the temptation to act like something that was drained out of a colorectal fistula, then we can both enter our homes justified.

Why? Because that person will, in turn, model good behavior to everyone who works for her or him - and those employees will know that it is good to work for an ethical, sensitive, and empowering manager, and they will take that into their own path to success - and the rest is evolution.

There are many of us who look at the current political situation - the endless lies and gaslighting, the normalization of casual hate, prejudice, and misogyny - and wonder only one thing... what to do? Some run for office, some go to demonstrations, call their congressmen, read all the newspapers and blogs...

And some of us have no taste, stomach, or talent for it. I'm not talking about sloth or apathy, I'm talking about the truth that we all have limitations. I have none of the requisite qualities necessary to become a political truncheon; but that doesn't mean that I don't live in the same fish tank, breathe the same liquid, and choke on the same poison.

I have one solution. It's not the only solution - not even close. It's also not a solution that will force anyone out of the seat of power, bring about an end to the systematic abuse of women in our society, or expedite the punishment of the guilty... but that doesn't make it not worth exploring.

If you have a skill, teach it to someone for free.

This is especially necessary if you are a writer. Because if you make it, it won't just be because you are great (though I am sure you are, each and every one of you, the reincarnation of Mavis Gallant) it will be because all of the gatekeepers opened the locks for you.

Anyone lucky - yes, lucky - enough to make a living as a writer has a list of people who recognized their talent, helped them hone their craft, gave them honest but compassionate feedback, introduced them to an agent, explained publishing to them, advised them on how to deal with editors - or network and studio executives - and perhaps taught them how to handle both success and failure with grace.

And if you were to share your knowledge of how those pins and barrels were made to turn for you, imagine how many might be able to walk into the promised land through a path you described. How many stories might see the light that may otherwise have not.

Every time you give knowledge away for free, every time you teach, every time you empower someone who is not, you are creating something that cannot be measured in terms of capital but is nevertheless a profoundly political act:

You are increasing the density of decency in the world.

Every time you are generous with knowledge that is considered privileged, you are not just saying that you have faith that the arc of the universe bends toward morality, you are becoming one of the billions of moving pieces whose trajectory defines that arc. Even more importantly, you are modeling kindness as a value.

The more we seed the world with the idea that empathy is not a hindrance to victory, but rather its vehicle - the more we declare through action that there is more to "winning" than profit and dominance - the more likely we are to create a majority for whom what is "cool" and "aspirational" is not for sale. Some of us stand up to bullies by quietly recruiting more and more into the ranks of warriors for that which is soft, and gentle, and far more necessary to the soul than "winning."

And trust me, I'm not advocating that you put your professors or this university out of business. If you are doing it right, your experience of a place like this will be irreproducible. I'm also not telling you to give your secrets to "the competition." What you bring to the page is the one thing you can't teach or give away; the only way to truly understand that is to put everything else on the table.

Some of you may now be saying "but what if I'm too busy changing the world through my amazing writing?" Then I would suggest you study the life of one of the most successful classical composers in history. A man whose voice dominated opera between the eighteenth and nineteenth century. A man who retired one of the wealthiest classical composers in history. A man who taught composition to Schubert, Liszt, and Beethoven.

His name is Antonio Salieri. His story is a cautionary tale that should be familiar to all you cultural studies double-majors who have been force fed Roland Barthes. Today, this man's name is known only because - a hundred and fifty years after his death - another artist wrote a grotesquely inaccurate script framing him for the murder of Mozart, holding him up as poster child for the sin of envy, and canonizing him as patron saint of mediocrity.

What happens to your work and your story in the ashes of time is completely beyond your control. The only thing that survives eternity is your place in an unbroken chain of acts that encourage others to surpass you. In the immortal words of Jedi master Yoda: "We are what they grow beyond, that is the true burden of all masters."

But ultimately, it's a little weird that you should be listening to me on this topic when, not one square mile from here there lived and worked a true warrior for social justice - a writer, musician, spoken-word performance artist, film-maker, pacifist, and humanist - who said it better, and far more succinctly than I ever could. A man who has been vilified by Fox News and many other standard-bearers of speaking-power-to-truth - and who was frequently accused of everything from mass murder to child molestation - for the crime of putting into the world such heresies as this one: "As human beings, our job in life is to help people realize how rare and valuable each one of us really is, that each of us has something that no one else has - or ever will have - something inside that is unique to all time. It's our job to encourage each other to discover that uniqueness and to provide ways of developing its expression."[1]

His name was, of course, Fred Rogers, and he remains one of my personal idols to this day because he talked the talk, walked the walk, endured the cruelty and ridicule of many with the humane smile of one who knows truth beyond reproach, and embodied day in and day out - without shame, or fear, or guilt - a reality that, sadly, grows more urgent with each passing day...

In this moment, there is nothing more revolutionary, counter-cultural, and just plain badass than simple human decency.

---

1   Rogers, Fred, *The World According to Mister Rogers* (New York, Hyperion, 2003), 137

THE LOST WILL AND TESTAMENT OF JAVIER GRILLO-MARXUACH

3/24/15

A t the risk of extreme arrogance, I would put the first season of *Lost* alongside any accomplishment in television drama, including those of the idols who made me want to work in the medium.

Even though I quit the show after its second season - never to watch it again until the series finale - I have never ceased to be fiercely proud, and defensive, of our accomplishments as a writing staff, and those of the show's creators.

If you are reading this, it might be because you asked me how it all began and I sent you here. Or it might be because - as still happens with depressing regularity - one of the show's detractors, be that a critic, or, more vexingly, someone who has just created a show and wants to make sure the media realizes that they are above making the mistakes we made (all the while cribbing our best moves) has come out purporting yet again to have some sort "proof" that "the writers of *Lost* did not know what they were doing."

Eleven years on, even with all the media coverage, pre- and post-mortem interviews, reviews, critiques, tributes, lookbacks, and "oral histories"... even though *Lost* might as well hold a record as the most over-documented series in the history of television, many still feel like a definitive version of how we made the show has yet to be told.

This is not that.

I'm writing down my recollections of the early days of *Lost* for profoundly selfish reasons. After eleven years, the story I am about to tell, hopefully for the last time, continues to hold a fascination for many. While I have been happy to tell it, and strive to do so with joy and gratitude for all that *Lost* did for me, there comes a time when the memories fade, and the instinct to embellish - to make oneself the hero of every encounter, and, to borrow a term, to "retcon" - takes over where reasonably factual recollection once stood.

What follows began as an on-the-record response to a journalist who reached out to me for background for a book on the current "Golden Age" of television. My selfish desire is to put this all down as I remember, then leave it for anyone who is interested to find so that I can stop telling the story... and in doing so, maybe someday revisit the series not through the lens of a participant, but that of a viewer who has never been asked - as I have a million times - "Did you have a plan?" or "Were you lying when you said in an interview that the writers knew what the island was? "What was JJ/Damon/Carlton like?" "Was it purgatory?" - and, of course, my personal favorite, "No, come on, really, was it purgatory?"

This is how it was for me, and - begging your indulgence - please know that we are each the protagonists of our own movie, even if we claim otherwise. If this contradicts the events of anyone else's movie, please take it as read that I have no scores to settle, no record to set straight, and no grudges to feed as far as the people with whom I worked.

This just happens to be the movie I was in, the scenes

in which I participated, and the plot in which I happened to be inserted as a featured player. If there were other movies playing at other theaters, movies with the same story but different scenes, then I offer no counter, just the hope that those movies were as good a ride as mine.

I owe the successful second half of my career to *Lost*, and I owe my employment on *Lost* to *America's Next Top Model*. In January of 2004, I was working on the United Paramount Network's low-rated - if much-loved by its writers - series *Jake 2.0*. Although we knew our show was not long for this Earth, we figured we would have a chance to wrap up our season with a proper finale.

That was until the network pre-empted us for a rerun of *America's Next Top Model*: a rerun that doubled the ratings of our previous original airing.

At 11:30 AM the following day, the Executive Producers of *Jake 2.0* received a call from the president of UPN. By 4:00 PM that day, our offices were packed and the writers were sent home.

I was now available to seek other employment.

Meanwhile, across town at ABC, network president Lloyd Braun took the ballsy step of green-lighting a two-hour pilot off an outline.

This part of the story is generally well known: at a corporate retreat in 2003, Braun pitched his development team the idea of doing *Survivor* meets *Cast Away* as a dramatic series. The first script generated for this came from writer Jeffrey Lieber and was called *Nowhere*.

Dissatisfied with Lieber's execution, Braun and company tasked JJ Abrams with working up an alternate take on his one-line high concept. Through ABC executive Heather Kadin, Damon Lindelof - then a producer on *Crossing Jordan* - was identified as a potential showrunner.

In very short order, Damon and JJ developed an outline which so blew Braun and his team away that they chose to strike while the iron was hot - and greenlight to film a pilot to be written by JJ and Damon based on the outline.

This was at a time of the year when most premises for network pilots - the scripts for the shows with which *Lost* would be battling for a spot on the network schedule in five months - had also been mulled over, outlined, considered and reconsidered, and rewritten and rewritten, with copious amount of input from the network and studios. The reason scripts get pored over with such a fine-toothed comb? Before everyone commits to spending millions on filming them, they need to know whether the pilot script described a series that can successfully sustain itself for years.

Damon and JJ now had the nigh-impossible task of not only delivering a great script based on their outline, but to also film that script, and chart the course of an ensuing series with no road map for its future, and no discernible plot engine for episode after episode other than "survival."

Along with Damon, JJ had also recruited *Alias* producers Jesse Alexander and Jeff Pinkner to help develop many of the elements that made it into that fateful outline. Though they were on *Alias* full time, Jesse and Jeff would occasionally return to *Lost* over the first season to consult on stories and concepts, and help with story breaks - later on, *Alias* would also lend us Drew Goddard to break and write an episode. The conceptual support provided by these two, especially during the early work on the pilot outline, earned Jeff and Jesse the credit of Executive Consultant on both pilot and series. In later seasons, Pinkner would even return to executive produce alongside Damon and Carlton Cuse.

At the time the pilot was being written, however, Jeff and Jesse were also needed on *Alias* - which was in production and on the air - especially with JJ shifting his energies toward co-writing and directing the *Lost* pilot. Though thrilled about taking a wild swing on a new project from the creator of *Alias*, the network was justifiably concerned.

In what was a pretty unorthodox move at the time, as JJ and Damon were beavering away on the first draft of the *Lost* pilot at various Starbucks locations around the city (it's hard to believe now, with JJ squiring the *Star Wars* franchise and Damon doing the same on a number of feature films as well as a prestigious HBO series, that such a scene could even be possible), ABC funded a small "think tank" of writers to work closely with them in narrowing down what the actual series would be...

And when my agent mentioned this to me, I didn't think that A. this crazy idea would ever get off the ground - I mean, greenlighting a pilot this late in the game off an outline? Insanity. - and B. that I would ever get the job anyway. (I had run into JJ a few times in my career - we were once speakers at a conference for magnet school students, for example - and I never got the sense that he was especially impressed with me, an impression bolstered by my inability to get so much as an interview on any Bad Robot shows in the past.)

That much said, time was of the essence now. *Lost* needed qualified writers with development and genre experience - and, to my very good fortune, I had become friends with Jesse Alexander outside of our work lives. He went to bat for me. After one meeting with a very overwhelmed-looking Damon, and a very - and very typically - cool and enthusiastic JJ, I had a spot in the think tank.

The think tank also included Paul Dini (of *Batman: The Animated Series*), Christian Taylor (who went on to run *Teen Wolf* and *eyeCandy*), and Jennifer Johnson (who went on to run *Cold Case*). Our job was to brainstorm elements that could become the show's mythology as well as the character backstories that would - eventually - become the majority of the flashbacks for the first season.

Basically, a *Lost* writers room existed parallel to the development of the pilot, working closely with the show's creators. Most days we would sit in conference with Damon for several hours and then work from his instructions as he left the room for rewriting, notes, casting, and so on. While the pilot was being filmed in Hawaii, we would do the same and pitch our ideas to him on the phone in between takes.

During these sessions - which began on February 24th of 2004, exactly one day before Damon and JJ finished writing their very first draft of the pilot - a lot of the ideas that became the show's mythology and format were discussed, pitched, and put into play for what would eventually become the series. Also, to be fair, more often than not, we were paving the way for the good ideas by coming up with a lot of bad ones.

Very bad ones.

On the first day alone, Damon downloaded on us the notion that the island was a nexus of conflict between good and evil: an uncharted and unchartable place with a mysterious force at its core that called humanity to it to play out a primal contest between light and dark.

In that meeting - we had an assistant taking the notes I am consulting as I write this - Damon also pitched out the idea of "The Medusa Corporation": a Rand Corporation-like entity that knew the nature of the island and had thus chosen it as a place in which to perform a series of behavior modification experiments in a series of scientific stations... and who had brought the polar bears in for these experiments.

The reason The Medusa Corporation was performing these experiments was that they had stumbled on an equation - much like the famed Drake equation, popularized by Carl Sagan in *Cosmos* and used to estimate the number of discoverable worlds holding life in the universe - which predicted the end of the world. By performing experiments in a place they knew as a crucible for extremes of human behavior - some of those experiments involving behavioral modification on polar bears - Medusa hoped to change humanity and avoid an impending armageddon.

Among the other core notions that came up on this very first day were the idea of the hatch (more about that in a moment), and the notion that Locke was a warped, frustrated man whose mystical experience as a result of the plane crash had brought him to see himself as an enlightened figure whose destiny was to be revealed on the island. The exact nature of his mystical experience, however, would not be decided until much, much later.

These ideas were in the DNA of *Lost* from jump street and were presented to us as take-off points from which to work out our brainstorms. The reason I bring this up is not to argue that we had a plan all along - although I suppose I could wave that notes document around and reasonably say, "See, our mythology was there from ground zero."

No, the reason I mention it is because one of the ongoing themes of this piece is that nothing springs fully formed from anyone's mind... not even something as seemingly magical as *Lost*, and the answer to the question of "Were we making it all up as we went?" is inextricably tied to this truth.

As much as many - fans, critics, and sometimes even those of us who create the stuff - want to believe in the possibility that greatness is *sui generis* (or conversely the cowboy myth that "We didn't know what we were doing - we were just kids with a dream and gosh darnit we pulled it off with spit and baling wire") both of these explanations rob us of the truth: inspiration is always augmented through improvisation, collaboration, serendipity, and plain, old, unglamorous Hard Work.

I will, however, strenuously make the point that the notes from our think tank prove beyond a shadow of a doubt that if we knew anything, we sure as shellac knew what the polar bear was doing on the island.

Also - and I present this as neither apology nor indictment - if the concepts described above seem thin to you, I have (in the time since *Lost* aired and I have found my services in demand by shows that seek to ape its success and methods) gone to work on piloted, ordered, serialized sci-fi shows with far less secure underpinnings than even what I just described. In one case, the creator and executive producers of a series that hoped to hire me answered my question of "So where are you going with this?" with "You worked on *Lost*, you tell us."

So, dear reader, if you have been privy to the widespread impression that we were making it up as we went and merely blundered onto great success - and feel shafted by that - you're not alone.

At this point in the story, I'm often asked the question of Jeffrey Lieber's script, *Nowhere*. Did we read it? Did Damon and JJ read it? Did we use it as a reference? Was it fair for the Writers Guild to grant Lieber a third of the created-by credit on *Lost*?

Having read up to this point, I can safely say that you now know as much about Jeffrey Lieber's script as I do today, and did at the time. Those of us in the think tank were told of its existence, but I truly do not know who else might have read it or when. I am therefore completely agnostic about its merits and have no opinion one way or the other about the WGA's ruling. I never saw the thing and the think tank never used it in its work: it was in the past by the time I got there, and we were moving forward at breakneck speed.

Lost was anything but fully-baked in late February of 2004. As has been reported elsewhere, one of the out-of-the-box ideas featured in both the greenlit outline and the first draft of the pilot was that Jack Shephard - the main character of the series that ultimately aired - was to be killed at the end of the first act by the mysterious smoke monster. At the time, the scuttlebutt around the office was that JJ had reached out to Michael Keaton, who had - at least in principle - agreed to appear in the pilot and even do press pretending that he was going to be a series regular, only to be killed fifteen minutes in.

The film *Executive Decision* - in which Steven Seagal appears to be the film's lead tough hombre until he sacrifices himself at the end of the first act in a "tough hombre handoff" to Kurt Russell - was often mentioned as a template for this kind of surprise, often alongside Samuel L. Jackson's untimely, and perhaps unintentionally hilarious, demise in Renny Harlin's *Deep Blue Sea*.

On our second day at work, JJ and Damon brought in numbered hard copies of the pilot for the think tank to read and on which to give feedback. My most salient note on the pilot was that murdering the one white male character with a discernible skillset that could serve to generate stories - at the very least Jack was a doctor - would not go over well with the network.

In truth, my response was a lot less politically correct, informed as it was by my decade-plus experience as a Puerto Rican working in Hollywood.

What I really said was "You can't kill the white guy."

As cool a piece of showmanship as killing Jack in the first act would have been, I had serious doubts as to whether American network television would welcome a show anchored by a warped, frustrated middle-aged guy with delusions of grandeur, or an overweight Mexican, or a reformed Iraqi torturer, or a southern-fried con artist whose skills would have been essentially useless in the wild, or a non-anglophone Asian couple, or a character who was likely to be played by an actress whose most salient speaking role up until then had been in a commercial for a late-night chat phone line in Vancouver.

But for Jack, *Lost* seemed to be a series populated entirely by supporting characters: at least by the standards of our medium.

One reason I was able to make the argument as phrased above was that, even at this early juncture, a lot of the actors who wound up on the show were already hovering around the project - we already had a good idea of the kinds of faces that would go with the names. As Damon and JJ worked on the pilot, pre-production was moving rapidly - even if all they had to go on was an outline and pieces of a work-in-progress script. The assumption had to be that the final script would not diverge tremendously from the greenlit outline so that locations could be scouted, sets built, and the major set pieces, such as the opening sequence depicting the crash of Oceanic 815, could be planned. It also helped that JJ could use the infrastructure Bad Robot had in place for *Alias* to help grease the skids.

So while we brainstormed, line producer Sarah Caplan was busily negotiating the purchase of an L-1011 fuselage and researching how to get it to Hawaii, and April Webster, who also cast *Alias*, was already using scenes from the script to find actors.

In spite of her relative lack of experience, Evangeline Lilly had already been identified as a potential Kate, the latest in a long line of JJ-discovered talent going back to Keri Russell and continuing with Jennifer Garner. Hurley had originally been conceived as a "receding hairline, short sleeves and tie" nebbish until JJ and Damon spotted Jorge Garcia in an episode of *Curb Your Enthusiasm*, and essentially wrote the role for him (even if, like Matthew Fox, he originally auditioned reading a monologue written for Sawyer). Terry O'Quinn had appeared in eighteen episodes of *Alias* and, at least by the time I got there, his participation as Locke was assumed to be fait accompli. There was certainly no discussion of any other actor playing the part in our room.

Now these were all great actors who would soon be playing characters that, in great part due to their interpretation, would become iconic... but the sad reality of American network television in 2004 was that shows needed competent, easily identifiable main characters with abilities that undeniably spoke to their leadership and heroism: and that was, most of the time, a handsome white guy with an advanced degree in criminology, law, or medicine... and an absurdly tragic backstory.

So when JJ and Damon returned from their first

network notes session with a slightly bemused expression, I asked how the notes session went. I was not shocked when Damon shrugged with a not inconsiderable amount of contempt for his unimaginative corporate overlords and reported that, "We can't kill the white guy."

This is also a long way of saying that multiple tracks of invention were running simultaneously and affecting one another - from production, to casting, to creative, and finally the studio and network's constantly shifting preferences for the series. A lot of different people were working very quickly to make JJ and Damon's vision a reality - some of them weighing in with input designed to make this vision more network friendly, or at least identifiable in their eyes as that rare beast known as "a TV show" - and JJ and Damon were working very quickly on their end to provide a vision which could be made reality.

While a lot of the accounts of *Lost*'s creation hinge on the question of whether we knew what the island was - and a lot of the criticism of the show centers around whether or not we had worked out the mythology in advance and whether or not we accurately represented to the press the extent of our preparation once the show became a success - few people ever ask if we knew the characters or had their stories worked out in advance. I find that curious.

Arguably, the reason audience members fell in love with *Lost* was as much, if not more, that they bonded with our ensemble as they were tantalized by the mysteries of the island. Much of our work in those early days came in the form of figuring out who those characters were, how they would interact in series, and how their stories could play out in relationship to one another.

Another factor that heavily affected the format and

presentation of both the character and mythological elements of *Lost* throughout its prehistory and first season is one of the essential truths of broadcast television to this day. Even though this seems incredibly counter-intuitive given what is successful and buzzworthy, network television was, and remains, extremely genre-averse.

Up until very, very recently - and by that I mean well into the early aughts - sci-fi shows were considered something of a ghetto, and the true wellsprings of "quality" writing in television were the ten o'clock police/lawyer/doctor shows. The prejudices of current high-level network execs, most of whom came up in the 90s, continue to reflect that upbringing - as does the lack of Emmy wins and nominations for a genre that represents a huge amount of the drama made for television today.

As a result, even though JJ and Damon had sold a show about a mysterious tropical island full of polar bears and patrolled by a free-roaming cloud of sentient smoke, we had to continually promise during the show's development, the filming of the pilot, and even well into the first and second season, that - at most - our sci-fi would be of a grounded, believable, Michael Crichton-esque stripe that could be proven plausible through extrapolation from hard science.

Of course, that was a blatant and shameless lie told to network and studio executives in the hopes that either blazing success or crashing failure would eventually exonerate us from the responsibility of explaining the scientifically accurate manner in which the man-eating cloud of sentient smoke actually operated. Nevertheless, the onus was on us to generate tons of exciting stories that could stand on their own without leaning too hard on genre, and in television there is only one way of doing that:

have great characters who are interesting to watch as they solve problems onscreen.

So, while we routinely discussed such genre questions as "what is the island?" we also asked ourselves "Who are these people, why were they on the plane, and why are they interesting company on a desert island?"

Up until May 2004, when the *Lost* pilot was screened for ABC and picked up to become a series - the writers genuinely believed that the show would be completely self-contained on the island. Based on that, we tried to break A and B stories around the *Lord of the Flies*/"How do you create a civilization when you are stranded with no hope of escape?" theme.

To make this premise work, we created extensively detailed character backstories which we hoped we could use as reference for why the castaways did what they did in the island. For weeks, each member of the think tank would be assigned one character, and in our time outside the room, we would come up with incidents in the characters' lives to pitch to one another. In the room, the think tank would then work with Damon, who would cherry-pick the events he found interesting, and we would round up the characters from there. More often than not, these would be the stories that the think tank writers wound up writing when they were assigned episodes come the series... which is how I wound up writing the Jack backstory episode "All the Best Cowboys Have Daddy Issues."

By the time the pilot was finished, we knew that Jack would be the overachieving son of a patrician, alcoholic doctor, haunted by having to betray his father... that Charlie's drug issues were fueled by the breakup of his band... that Locke would be played as a shaman on the island but a sad, frustrated drone in his real life... that Sayid's dark romantic demeanor was the result of being separated from the love of his life... that Jin had made a Faustian bargain with Sun's billionaire father in order to marry her, but that the bargain had twisted his soul and forced her to secretly learn English as an exit strategy... that Boone and Shannon were on the plane as a result of Boone's having to rescue her from a rich, abusive lover... that Sawyer's entire life had been destroyed by a con artist, and that the act had driven him to become a con artist himself. The backstories flowed with surprising ease from the hints and actions of the characters in the pilot - JJ and Damon's writing gave us a fertile field in which to play, and the possibilities for our castaways' histories outside the island seemed endless. Too bad they were never going to be seen on the screen - only spoken of.

So, while this approach yielded some very interesting character possibilities, it still didn't solve one major problem... most of the "island stories" we came up with were pretty lame. The scintillating B. and C. stories we came up with during this period included "Shannon trades sexual favors for sunscreen, which has rapidly become the most prized commodity on the island," "Sawyer builds a still," "Vincent (Walt's dog) becomes Cujo," and, my personal favorite, "Hurley eats a bad coconut" (which, weirdly, was the only one of these three to ever see the light of day as a runner in a season one episode in which he approaches Jack with complaints of gastrointestinal distress). You sow the field of good ideas with the dead bodies of bad ideas.

It was also during these sessions that we came up with many other notions which would eventually come to fruition in series: Charlie's drug withdrawal, Shannon's insulin dependency and how it leads to Sawyer's torture by Sayid, the struggle to save a man whose seat was lodged in a high tree after the crash (an idea that did not emerge until season 2), the concept that the island could summon the presence of figures from the castaways' past (like Hurley's friend from the psych ward and Jack's father), the possibility of introducing the tail section survivors as a way to add conflict to the series, and the "jungle creeps," mysterious inhabitants of the island who put a ringer in the corps of survivors after the crash in order to find out our secrets.

The "jungle creeps," who eventually became "The Others," are a good example of our struggle to find viable stories when the network continually pushed us to deliver a "grounded" and "believable" show that went to sci-fi as little as possible. When we first ran the idea of the "jungle creeps" by ABC, they balked, feeling that it was too early to introduce other participants to the drama of survival when we already had fifteen ensemble mouths to feed.

Additionally, they felt that explaining a mysterious presence on the island - of people who could pass for modern-day castaways - was a bridge too far. The compromise struck in series was that The Others would not be introduced until about halfway into the first season.

The problem of the network's belief that we were going to deliver a show whose science fiction was "completely grounded in reality" was a constant issue in these sessions, as was the question of whether the episodes would be serialized or stand alone. The final result of all of this was a now widely-circulated - and widely used as proof of our incompetence/malfeasance/deception about our intentions - format document, dated May 5, 2004.

In this document Damon and JJ pitch the notion of *Lost*

as a mystery/genre series in which every episode would feature personal stories of survival (sunscreen as currency, the dying marshal, a sickness that threatens to wipe out the survivors, a cache of firearms is discovered on the island, Michael and Sun develop a relationship that ignites Jin's jealousy, an inability to find potable water, an exodus to an inland camp of caves which winds up dividing the castaways) as well as much wilder science-fictional ideas which we hoped we could use to sell the premise of the island's preternatural abilities (intelligent dolphins appear in the bay and attack our castaways, a solar eclipse that lasts for forty-eight hours, ravenous soldier ants destroy our food supply, Sayid fights a giant snake, a submarine runs aground on the barrier reef).

Needless to say, even at this late time and with all this lead time and story development, the show came across as more than a little bit schizophrenic... rich characters struggling for survival... and the occasional science fictional lark. In spite of that, JJ and Damon, along with the rest of the crew, had delivered a pilot so spectacular that the show's chances were undeniable. A viable series format had to be developed.

As we waited to find out our fate, we began to fully beat out what would eventually become episode 2 of the series, "Tabula Rasa." This early attempt at a full story break was an interesting test of our premises of what the show was and could be. While we knew that we would have to eventually unpack such series-wide elements as the provenance of the polar bear and the French Woman's broadcast, the true meaning of the "Black Rock" (that one we would not figure out until well into season one) and the Medusa Corporation and The Others (as of the May 5th document, they had officially been renamed from the, admittedly, Sid and Marty Krofftian "jungle creeps"), we were under strict orders to deliver a solid island A story that had nothing to do with the science-fictional elements of the show so as to prove to the network that it was possible to be *Lost* without being all about the smoke monster.

The truly gripping notion of having to euthanize a dying castaway became the center of this episode break - and made for an outstanding A story with a lot of self-evident scene possibilities. As we tried to graft to that a spine-tingling runner about digging latrines, and a destined-for-must-see-TV discussion about the funeral procedure for those who died in the plane crash, one undeniable truth kept coming up, a truth that we kept skirting for three months of brainstorming but had never embraced...

If the pilot featured flashbacks to the plane before the crash - and the context they provided for the island story was such a great source of contrast and revelation - and if we spent so much time developing the backstories of these characters - why not make that a part of the series?

Wouldn't it be great if we could see Kate's arrest by the marshal, and maybe their previous Kimble/Gerard relationship as a contrast to her trying to pretend that she didn't know him?

It is difficult to imagine that for so long - when they were part of the pilot, and frequently discussed in the think tank, and when they were so clearly the pivotal thematic lever of the series - the flashbacks were not considered as being of the essence to the show. Instead, the device was sort of tacitly agreed to have been a thematic grace note that would remain unique to the pilot and not be used in series.

Now, however, as we truly tried to put our ideas into practice, the episodic format finally took shape around the notion that "flashbacks are there to demonstrate what you are in the island is a contrast to what you were in your other life." This conceit became the theme of *Lost*, our central concern in the development of the stories, and the glue that held seasons of the show together.

We had been so concerned about how much sci-fi we could or couldn't get into the stories, and about whether or not the series could be serialized or not, that we didn't stop to consider that the stories we had created for our characters could not only carry the freight of our narrative, but also create a crucial thematic counterpoint. Equally importantly, we didn't realize until very late that the flashbacks would provide visual opportunities different from the dust and grime of a survival existence. And, yes, by that, I mean "flashbacks allowed us to put the characters in clean, fashionable clothes and spectacular hair."

It's shocking, in hindsight, that it took so long for us to get there, but thank YHWH that we did.

Obviously, the idea of flash-forwards - and the "flash-sideways" I often heard about from fans of the show in subsequent seasons - were much, much later ones that were developed as a way to generate further story as the show progressed into maturity.

I can't opine too much about these ideas, as I was not present when it was decided to put them into play, but can say with absolute certainty that they were not part of our discussion either in the think tank or the writers room in seasons one and two. As with the flashbacks, they most likely became very good ways of continuing to explore character outside of the confining paradigm of island survival.

Long before the flashbacks were finally set as a keystone of the format of the show, the idea had been conceived and settled on that each episode should represent a single day on the island. Indeed. This shows up at the top of the first page of our 2/24/04 writers meeting notes.

To some degree, the one-day-per-episode structure combined with the flashbacks provided the best of all worlds: of course the show would be serialized, the time frame of one episode per day demanded it, but this also allowed us to appease the desire for self-contained stories with beginnings, middles, and ends... every next day in series time, someone new would pick up the narrative freight in a flashback-driven tale showcasing the dichotomy between who they were in real life and who they were on the island.

With this construction, we could continue to address holdover threads from the previous episodes (in episode two, this became the question of whether the survivors who heard the French Woman's message would share that information with the other survivors and risk crushing their hopes for a rescue) while still claiming we were not wholly serialized.

Even as we came to these breakthroughs, ABC continued to vacillate about what they wanted *Lost* to be. The biggest reason for this was a change at the top ranks of the network. Sometime during all of this, Lloyd Braun - who had been willing to take a wild and wooly swing on the insanity that was *Lost* and its accelerated development process - was replaced as president of ABC by Stephen McPherson.

Previously, McPherson held the post of president of

ABC Studios. This meant that mere months ago, when the president of the network shocked the studio by saying "I've just greenlit a pilot based on an outline, and you are going to produce it, and no one's sure what the series is, and it's going to cost ten million dollars," it was McPherson who got the call. As head of the network's primary corporate sibling, McPherson had to accept the gamble even though he felt it foolhardy.

To say that McPherson did not share Braun's "seat of your pants" spirit of adventure vis-a-vis *Lost* would be an understatement, at least based on what JJ and Damon shared with us in the think tank. To us it seemed like the new management at ABC was actively trying to hedge their bet and mitigate the huge investment they made in the *Lost* pilot if either it didn't go to series or if it went to series and flopped (though I would go on to be a Supervising Producer on the series, no one ever gave me an exact figure of the final cost of the pilot episode - estimates vary between ten and thirteen million dollars).

At one point between the delivery of our format document and the decision to pick up the show, the network floated several ideas, including that we reshoot a more conclusive end to the pilot film and air it as a "backdoor pilot" - which would only go to series if airing it as a TV movie yielded spectacular ratings.

Another option presented was that we could do *Lost* as a six-episode miniseries. Bad Robot balked at all of these.

By the time the show was picked up, we knew - at least in theory - that we had an episodic structure that could sustain at least dozens of stories without giving up the secrets of the island - such as we had developed them. The idea of dedicating one of each of our first set of episodes to a major character, focusing on their backstory and some struggle on the island, made us see the longevity of the series beyond a "case of the week" (or rather an "island problem of the week"). The serialized format, then, was ultimately something that we simultaneously insisted on but also sort of snuck past the goalie by finding a middle ground where stories could also be self-contained.

This is how the battle of twenty-two-episode-year network television is fought and won. Not by relying on lone geniuses to come up with everything (though they sometimes do), but by relying on the geniuses to inspire their staffs (which hopefully comprise a few geniuses) with great ideas that generate tons of further ideas - some good, some bad, and some downright insane - and then cherry-pick the best of the best and integrate them into the show.

On my first meeting at *Lost*, Damon Lindelof was introduced to me as THE showrunner of the project. It was in this capacity that Damon functioned even as he collaborated with JJ in co-writing the script - and even though JJ directed the pilot and his production company produced the series.

Thus, on Damon fell the monolithic task to set the tone for not only how we would explain the mysteries of the island, but also of how we would negotiate all the creative forces tugging at the series. Even in our autocratic system in which the showrunner is believed to be the ultimate authority, it's still a collaborative process in which a lot of people - many of them having greater power, especially in the case of a first timer like Damon - generate, challenge, and refine ideas until the showrunner, often with studio and network holding veto power, decides which are worthy and which are not.

The creative rhythm of *Lost* through these gestational phases, as well as the bulk of the first season, then, was dictated almost exclusively by Damon's personal tastes and sensibilities. Damon's oft-stated-in-the-writers-room belief, for example, that dysfunctional relationships between parents and children are the core of all good drama is clearly evident throughout the series.

In this capacity, Damon also faced the daunting task of setting the pace at which we were to reveal the mysteries of the island. This was made all the more difficult for him in the first season - and then for years to come in showrunning collaboration with Carlton Cuse - not only by the number of other influencers in the kitchen (Bad Robot and JJ, ABC Studios, and ABC Network) but also by not knowing just how long the show would last.

This speaks directly to the notion of "Did we know what we were doing or did we just make it up as we went along?"

There's two answers to that...

Answer number one is - REALLY? Chill the fuck out already.

Seriously, time is linear and even God - who took seven days from when he invented light to when he decided that there could be people in there once he had separated the seas from the lands so that there was a dry spot to stand on - appears to have been making it up as he went along.

I mean honestly, why would an omniscient deity not realize until well after completing the act of creation that Adam might get lonely and need a mate? And why did he make Eve from Adam's rib? That seems like ret-conning of the most egregious order. This God guy seems like a worse improviser than the writers of *Lost*!

Here's answer number two...

As questions of mythology and backstory came up during the development of *Lost*, Damon and the staff -

first in the think tank and later in the writers' room for the series - would come up with explanations. The ones Damon liked just enough to not dismiss outright would be discussed at greater length and eventually, something would become a kind of operating theory. Damon would eventually declare, "It's going to be that unless someone can beat it." When we finally refined these ideas to the point where Damon was OK putting them on screen - committing to them as canon - then we would incorporate them into the show.

For example - even though we assumed from jump street that the polar bears had been brought to the island as part of the Medusa Corporation's work - there was also a very strong drive from Damon and JJ to advance the story that Walt was a powerful psychic. This explained, for example, the bird hitting the window in the episode "Special." Walt-as-psychic would also help us explain why The Others had such an interest in Walt and would ultimately kidnap him.

Although the genre-averse Powers That Be at network and studio were resolutely opposed to the science-fictional idea of a psychic boy who could manifest polar bears on a tropical island through the strength of will alone, Damon and JJ nevertheless gave themselves a backdoor into this area by putting the bear in a comic book that appeared both in the pilot and thereafter in series.

Frankly, it's hard for me to look at an episode like "Special" and not completely take from it that Walt is a powerful psychic who manifested the polar bear in order to test his father's love once and for all... but the execution of the episode apparently left plenty of wiggle room to give us plausible deniability - even as Damon would regularly come into the writers' room, throw up his arms and declare ,"Of course Walt's psychic."

In other cases, these things would come in through back doors and leave the same way very quickly. There was a time when - in order to appease the network's fear of sci-fi - the polar bear would simply be explained away as having been on the plane as freight. Needless to say, this idea came... and then went.

A good example of something that was never explained but for which there existed an internal explanation was the smoke monster. In think tank, we imagined it as a "security system" (which eventually became Rousseau's line) and a sort of mechanism of judgment that policed the island on behalf of the strange powers that ran the place and called out the good and evil in humanity to come. As the smoke monster would come and go through the first season - and, for example, have a face-off with Locke but "decide" to not kill him - we would say that the smoke monster possessed an intuitive psychic ability, like the sentient ocean in *Solaris*, and would be able to look into the souls of its prey in order to determine further action.

Up until the time when I left the show, this idea - and variations on it - were the common language of the writers when discussing the monster, but as far as I know, this explanation was never expressed in series because Damon never became fully comfortable with it. Again, this was partially because in the early days, any explanation that felt too fanciful would be kiboshed by the network. Since ABC seemed comfortable in having the monster without us actually explaining it, leaving well enough alone seemed a better course of action than to risk the network pulling at strands that would take apart even larger swaths of our story sweater.

We worked under this construct - "this is the explanation until someone beats it" - during most of the first season, being careful to dollop the mythology very sparingly while trying to keep the show grounded in the rich characters we had created. When the show became an undeniable hit and moved into its second season - and we had to show what was in the hatch once and for all - it became necessary to take all of those ideas out into the sun. With success, we were freer to explore a lot of the sci-fi we had thus far kept beneath the surface... but not as free as one might imagine.

Much of the fun camaraderie of the writers' room involved trying to "beat it" - spending our time straining to come up with increasingly byzantine ways in which we could dethrone the accepted wisdom with an idea that was not only great but also tied together all the extant plot and character strands. It was rare to succeed, but occasionally during the run of the first two seasons, someone would, in fact, come in with something so undeniable that it would supersede whatever was already in the show's zeitgeist as The Truth.

The strange case of the hatch may be the best example during the prehistory and first season of *Lost* of how the exchange of ideas between Damon, JJ, the writing staff, and the rest of our production and broadcast partners truly functioned. Because JJ's calling card back then was the whole concept of the "mystery box" - I won't bother to explain, he guest-curated an entire issue of *Wired* Magazine on the topic, the Bad Robot website sells limited edition "Mystery Boxes" based on the one from JJ's childhood, and frankly, if you have cared about this topic enough to read this far, you most likely already know the theory - he wanted the hatch in the pilot, even though no one knew what would be in it.

JJ was more than happy to punt the decision as to what would actually be inside the hatch to the writers' room because of his deeply felt conviction that the mystery was as good a journey as the reveal and would be so tantalizing it would keep the audience clamoring - even if the subject to be eventually revealed was not forethought. It was at that point that I first heard Damon articulate - wisely, and for reasons of self-preservation and sanity - the one hard and fast rule that he lived by for the entire first season. He would not put anything on screen that he didn't feel confident he could explain beforehand.

So the reason the hatch doesn't come up until the end of the tenth episode of the series ("All the Best Cowboys Have Daddy Issues") - even though JJ was stumping for it since before the pilot was written - was because Damon didn't fully believe in any of the ideas presented to him for what was there.

As a writers' room, and a think tank before that, we kept pitching possibilities, but nothing we threw out ever overrode Damon's concern that if we shat the bed on that reveal, the audience would depart in droves. The hatch was pitched as a gateway to a frozen polar bear habitat, the mouth of a cave full of treasure that would so entrance the castaways with dreams of avarice that Jack would ultimately be forced to seal it shut with dynamite, the door to a bio-dome whose inhabitants could only breathe carbon dioxide, and even a threshold to an Atlantis-style lost civilization.

I believe that my idea was that it led into the conning tower of a nuclear submarine that had run aground and been buried in an epic mudslide (I thought this could be a rich area for stories about salvaging equipment, and loose nukes, and such things).

As we trudged through the first half of season one, Damon rushed into the writers room one day with an uncharacteristic bounce in his step and declared that, "Inside the hatch there's a room with a guy in it and if he doesn't press a button every 108 minutes, the world will end."

It was a brilliant idea that he felt had legs and could be exploited for story mileage... of course, when we asked why this byzantine mechanism was necessary, the explanation was a lot more diffuse: it had to do with the exotic source of energy at the core of the island that caused all the other trouble faced by the castaways... at least until someone else figured out how to beat it. Thus armed with an operating theory with which Damon was comfortable, we soldiered on, put the discovery of the hatch into episode ten... and JJ finally got his mystery box.

This was Damon's response to - and ultimate compromise with - the whole construct of the mystery box. Damon didn't want to risk letting the audience down by promising something he couldn't deliver, so rather than fight the mysteries, he would merely defer them until an explanation could be added to the nimbus of ideas that already existed around the show. It's a good example of the collaborative relationship that developed between him and JJ both in the pre-history of the project and through the first part of the first season.

To many, all that I have already written may still not answer the question of "Did we know what we were doing, or were we just making it up as we went along?"

The truth is complicated, isn't it, dear reader? And it's only going to get more so...

The idea that there is a simple truth about the creation

of *Lost* also begs two additional questions... did we ever know what the island was? And was it purgatory?

If that's what you are here to find out, let me dispense with those quickly, as you probably feel like I have already wasted enough of your time.

As I described before, there was definitely a sort of "operational theory" for what the island would be - it was liked by some and loathed by others - and since Damon and Carlton chose not to say it out loud in the series finale, I won't presume to do it for them. Suffice it to say there was a concrete reason that we openly discussed on several occasions about why the island had an exotic source of power in its core that was able to wreak such miracles as time travel, the motion of the island, and somehow connect with selected people on a psychic level.

On question number two. It is not purgatory. It was never purgatory. It will never be purgatory.

Even after watching the series finale following a four-year absence from any exposure to the show, it was pretty clear to me that only after clearing up whatever insanity was happening on the island did Jack die... and then found himself in a pan-denominational spiritual halfway house where his father's spirit explained that - because the events of the island were so significant to the ensemble of *Lost* - they had all been brought here to wait for one another so that they would all ascend together. Frankly, I found it to be a nice spiritual grace note, but it most certainly was not a confirmation that the island was purgatory.

There, now you know. Go with God.

Of course, all these answers just keep causing that one question to rear its ugly head once more: "Did we really know what we were doing, or were we just making it up as we went?"

As with all other shows, the influx of talent into the writers room during the transition from pilot to series caused a lot of change, and questioning of the ideas with which the show came into being. On most shows, this process usually happens in apropos of a series bible written by the show's creator in close conjunction with their production company, studio, and network.

In our case, it was an extraordinary pilot film, a profoundly weird series format document/sales pitch that was obsolete before it left the offices of Bad Robot, a lot of disparate ideas that had been pitched at different times to network and studio over the course of five months of rolling series development, a sheaf of story and character pitches, and assorted notes from the think tank sessions... not to mention the contents of Damon Lindelof's brain: where many of these ideas had already coalesced as canon, many were in the process of being evaluated for their worth, and many were to die on the vine.

The writers room with which *Lost* would begin its first season was a wonderful collection of massively talented writers. It was also a very different room from that with which we would end the season - and I would describe that subsequent room in the same glowing terms.

That none of the inaugural staff - aside from me - survived the inevitable, and oftentimes unfair, adjustments that shows have to make in their personnel in order to find the right creative mix doesn't diminish their accomplishments. It was this writers room that, under Damon's leadership, crafted the first ten episodes of *Lost*. This first batch of episodes arguably cemented from the success of the pilot an enduring base of both audience support and critical approval that would set the tone for the show's enduring appeal.

These writers - the aforementioned Paul Dini, Jennifer Johnson, and Christian Taylor, now joined by co-Executive Producer David Fury, writer/producers Lynne Litt, and Kim Clements, and staff writer Monica Macer, assisted by future episode writers Matt Ragghianti and Dawn Lambertsen Kelly, and script coordinator Brent Fletcher - began on *Lost* the arduous process that all shows have to endure throughout their existence: turning mere ideas into drama.

Again, the answer to the question "Did we know what we were doing, or were we just making it up as we went along?" hits a logical snag here. *Lost* was not the first - nor the second or third - television series in existence to strand a cast of beautiful people, some with professional skills and some with shady pasts, on a deserted island. Sherwood Schwartz did it for laughs in the sixties with *Gilligan's Island*. Rod Serling did it for polemic, socially relevant drama in the early seventies with *The New People*. Hell, there was a show on German television in 2004 called *Verschollen* ("Forgotten") that dealt with survivors of a plane crash trying to live together on an island without hope of rescue - and even a YA series called *Flight 29 Down*, developed around the same time as *Lost*, that explored the premise, only with much younger characters.

All of these shows had ideas and notions, and characters, and maybe even a "plan" that described seasons worth of story: but the relative quality of all these projects did not hinge on the quality of their long-term strategy, but rather the quality of the translation of whatever thoughts the writers had from concept, to script, and to film.

That's what writers' rooms do: they take something like "Fifteen people with reams of variably canonical backstory that has been discussed over a period of months are stranded on a desert island where a mysterious organization conducted exotic experiments and will face a number of episodic challenges even as they are threatened by a violent group of inhabitants who are clearly not natives, but rather a coordinated and technologically advanced group of people with a habit of kidnapping gifted children" and turn it into an hour's worth of drama about people with rich inner lives and divergent opinions about how to live them figuring it out both against and alongside one another.

As a result, one could easily make the argument that we were, in fact, making it up as we went. "One" could also present the amount of change, refinement, and expansion that our core ideas underwent once the colloquium of writers went to work on them as proof.

In fact, let me present one case study that illustrates just that with one of the most shocking revelations of the series...

The idea that Locke was in a wheelchair was so late an addition to his episode that the entire story once existed without it. Even though we knew from the very first day that Locke's arc would be that of a warped, frustrated middle-aged man who, feeling that his survival was a mystical revelation, would recast himself as a sort of shamanistic badass on the island, the wheelchair was almost an afterthought.

The original story break for that episode focused on Locke being a meek, if physically able, office drone whose hopes and dreams had all fizzled out and he was trapped in a loser job where he was mercilessly abused and passed over by entitled, supercilious, younger co-workers. The original story break ended with Locke - who had bragged to his office rivals about embarking on the adventure of a lifetime - alone and miserable in a bus heading away from an outback tourist trap... realizing that his dreams of being a great adventurer were just that.

It was not until the episode had been plotted that Damon rushed into the writers room and pitched his overnight brainstorm that there should be a Sixth Sense-like twist... that Locke should be sitting in all of his scenes... and it's not until the end that we realize he was in a wheelchair all along, adding a layer of cruelty and poignancy to the abuse and skepticism he suffered from his co-workers...

And creating the shocking, series-defining reveal that the island had healed Locke and his transcendence may have been the product of a higher cosmic force at work on the island!

Overnight brainstorms were not unusual for Damon, who tended to come up with his best ideas when given a creative foundation, and then some time outside of the intellectual blood sport/competitive group therapy of the writers room to cogitate. It was in much the same way that he came up with the idea that Jack's father's casket would be on the plane, but his body would not be found - leading to occasional appearances on the island by his ghost.

The episode's writer, David Fury, initially argued against the Locke-in-a-Wheelchair twist. He held fast to the contention that he had already rendered a very Willy Loman-esque version of the story where Locke was a truly tragic figure. In David's arguments, the wheelchair twist was a kind of supernatural crutch that robbed the character of a pathos that felt lived-in and real.

Being showrunner, Damon eventually prevailed. Being a consummate professional and an exceptional artist,

Fury rendered the story so well that he was not only able to deliver the twist, but also overcome his objections to bring to Locke all the Willy Loman-esque tragedy he saw in the story before it went supernatural. As I said before, Locke-in-a-Wheelchair was widely seen as the turning point when *Lost* went from being a "hit pilot premiere" to being a "hit show." That episode - "Walkabout" - made our buzz go critical, and was also the source of an Emmy nomination for David.

What I just described was only one of a continuum of very interesting, ongoing, moments in which improvisation - coupled with a strong conceptual foundation of previously generated ideas - provided crucial watershed events for the series. Making these brainstorms happen was our job as a writers room, after all.

The shortest version of this type of event? One afternoon, Damon rushed into the writers room and asked to no one in particular "So what is 'The Black Rock'?"

Paul Dini lifted his head from his sketch pad (he was and is an accomplished doodler) and plainly stated "It's an eighteenth-century sailing ship that got beached on the island."

Damon exclaimed something to the effect of "Sold!" and quickly left the room: a new piece of canon born from raw improvisation colliding with something that had been planted in the pilot script months before.

I would be remiss if I didn't mention David Fury - Emmy nomination notwithstanding - as one of the unsung MVPs of the first season. The episode explaining Hurley's backstory, for example, did not come until late in the season, when David cracked it and provided the series with one of its most enduring motifs.

For most of season one, none of us could create a past that fit the tremendous charm that Jorge Garcia brought to the role of Hurley. Everything we came up with seemed to diminish the character that was actively evolving out of the lovely alchemy between the writers inspiration and the actor's interpretation of our work. For a long time, we had the idea that Hurley's real secret was that - because he was such an amiable sort - he was the world's most successful repo man and had been in Australia to repo a wayward tech millionaire's yacht. Hurley's "mutant ability" in this version of his story was that through his unassuming, best-friend-to-the-world demeanor, he could talk anyone out of anything.

Needless to say, no one could make that story work - and we REALLY tried. Damon eventually came up with the idea of Hurley winning the lottery, and the importance of the numbers became part of the story during a separate lunchtime conversation between him, Fury and JJ (whose visits to the show grew fewer and farther between). Believe it or not, the numbers were not part of the series mythology until well into the first season, although Damon was obsessed with the number 23 and the way it keeps popping up in the world.

So in this episode, we not only nailed down a backstory for Hurley that yielded episodic story fodder for years to come, but also, once the idea of the numbers manifested (and received its maiden voyage in a script once again written by David Fury, this time in collaboration with Brent Fletcher) the staff took the idea and ran with it. We not only presented the numbers everywhere we could, but also retrofitted them into what eventually became known as "The Valenzetti Equation" - the Drake-like construct that predicted the end of the world.

Again, this is a good example of how through improvisation a new idea fits perfectly with existing concepts and melds seamlessly into the texture of the series.

Another great idea that developed on the fly during the sweep of the first season was the notion that all our characters had met or somehow crossed paths during their flashbacks. This eventually became a crucial part of the series - that the world of *Lost* was one of ongoing connections between disparate people whose lives were on a path that would eventually reveal a common destiny - but it was certainly not in the original designs.

That literally came out of us thinking during the earliest episode breaks that, "Wouldn't it be neat if, when we flash back to someone at the airport, you can see someone else from the cast in the background doing something interesting?"

That notion eventually landed as one of the thematic pillars of the series. During the first season, it was a fun challenge to see just how creatively we could get the stories to merge... and because of that, eventually, Anthony Cooper became Sawyer's "Sawyer" and, later, Claire became Jack's half sister.

Once one great idea takes root, it leads to many others, and the job of the room is to follow the options and see where they take you.

There are also lot of things that developed long after I left the show, things that - when mentioned to me by friends still on the series, or fans whom I befriended during my time there - often made me go "huh?"

For example, while the idea was that the island called out to people and brought them in as part of a greater

Manichean conflict, I didn't once in two years and change hear the name "Jacob" or "the man in black." The idea that people were being recruited to come to the island as part of this greater agenda was never brought up during my time on the show, even though by all accounts it eventually became the crux of the series' final arc.

Presumably, as the length of the series increased, the writers needed to find ways to turn mere concepts into dramatic constructs... preferably with the ability to say dialogue.

Also, when I finally revisited the show after four years away, my initial response to the plot of the series finale was "why's Henry Gale still on this show and how did he become the most important man in the universe?"

So, just as most characters don't take on a life of their own until after the actors have brought their skills and interpretation to the table, there are few drawn-in-advance plans for series television - well or poorly sketched out - that survive the crucible of the writers room intact. Why hire a group of geniuses at great expense, to brainstorm and execute ideas, if you already know exactly what everything is and where it's supposed to go?

The *Lost* writers room, especially at this early stage, was a churlish and unwieldy beast. Big personalities, big ideas, and even bigger opinions. Not everybody played well together, not everybody took disagreement in stride, and it was often very difficult to get the ducks to quack in unison - or to agree that the word "quack" was a good representation of the vernacular - much less swim in a row.

Wresting consensus from this hydra would have been a job of work for the most hardened of showrunners. For a first-timer such as Damon, the room's natural tendency to argue everything until sternly being told otherwise - and then continue until threatened with outright extinction - was a source of much stress and anxiety.

As the series went into the day-to-day, week-to-week, grind of producing scripts and episodes with air date deadlines looming, the rigors of leading the production in Hawaii all the way from the writers office in Burbank - even with a magnificent producing director like Jack Bender at the helm along with producer Jean Higgins in Hawaii, the showrunner is expected to be the lead creative voice in the series - as well as JJ's mounting absence (it was always understood that he would not be a day-to-day presence in the series, but his quick acquisition of the directing assignment on *Mission: Impossible 3* made for a much faster departure than any of us expected - the *Lost* pilot, it seems, was a cracking directing sample, perfect to land the job on a Hollywood franchise tentpole), the strain on Damon was rapidly becoming a problem that would have to be addressed.

As early as the production of our sixth or seventh episode - shortly before *Lost* premiered - a search seemed to be going on for a showrunner who could come in and lighten some of Damon's load to allow him to do what he did best: be the lead creative voice of *Lost*.

For a few weeks, the names of potential candidates would come and go. Jeff Pinkner - who, as I mentioned before, would eventually sign up to executive produce later in the show's run - was one of these names. He was already in the Bad Robot family, was already a consultant on *Lost*, and worked on *Alias* just across the way from the offices of *Lost*. This arrangement, however, would not be feasible - in the best of times, neither *Alias* nor *Lost* were the sort of productions that could be executive-produced on a part-time basis, and we were in crisis.

Around the same time, John Eisendrath (a successful and well-regarded showrunner who had also worked on *Alias*, was then working on pilots with Bad Robot, and today runs *The Blacklist*) came in to watch the inner workings of *Lost*. All I know is that after a morning watching our writers room work the massive patchwork of fifteen series leads, flashbacks, and a not-entirely-developed and potentially science-fictional continuity, Eisendrath stood up from the couch, made a funny remark about the enormity of the task ahead, bid us farewell, and was never heard from again.

At the same time, Damon was in conversations with Carlton Cuse, who had hired him for his first network writing job on *Nash Bridges*, which Carlton had created, and whom he viewed as a mentor.

By the time Carlton came to work full-time on *Lost* - late September of '04, as I was outlining "All the Best Cowboys Have Daddy Issues" and as the room was about to launch the story break for "Whatever the Case May Be" - ABC had spent millions advertising the show, the critics had weighed in and anointed us one of the chosen, and sustained, pop culture-defining success seemed imminent... but all of this early promise could have just as easily turned to failure had the show imploded creatively.

Damon has been very frank in interviews about his state of mind during this time in the history of *Lost*, and I do not feel comfortable speaking for him. Here's what I witnessed and was told by him at the time: he paid a steep price to bring about the chemical reaction that resulted in the show's amazing premiere and first run of episodes.

To this day, I have great sympathy for Damon's plight: he had thrust upon him the stewardship of what became a highly profitable, network-defining franchise, with a billion moving parts and stratospheric stakes at a very early moment in his career. At the time, all I wanted was for him to stop wrestling the pack of black dogs running around his brain - especially the anxiety over not having the goods to back up the dramatic promises we had made - and relish the scope of his considerable accomplishment.

Through the first season of *Lost*, I was never anything less than confident that - with Damon's lead and the creative team we had in place - it was more than possible to present the audience with answers derived from our work and satisfy their hunger for the mysteries we had established. Perhaps that Damon couldn't share that confidence - and that it seemed to torture him on both an emotional and physical level - is the ultimate answer to those who believe that we never had a plan and were just making it up as we went.

Let me be absolutely clear on this, because Lindelof and *Lost* bashing remain to this day something akin to an Olympic sport. The man is every bit the genius he has been hyped to be. If you feel that not all of his work reflects this truth, I would ask, "Whose does who works at the pace of production - and with the levels of interference foisted on - film and television writers?"

Take this to the bank: in my years in television, I have rarely, if perhaps ever, met as uncannily gifted a spinner of yarns and creator of intrigue as Damon Lindelof.

Also, while I suppose that Damon and I remain reasonably cordial - I mean, it's been years since we last crossed paths, but that last time he didn't take a swing at me or anything - he remains first and foremost my former employer. I am certain that the email and phone number I have for him have been changed in the wake of his massive successes in the years since, and, even if they hadn't, I would not give them to anyone whose only recourse is to ask me for them.

Also, I can't get your spec script to Damon... or your story idea for *The Leftovers*... or your Dharma Initiative logo-shaped artisanal lolly-pops. I can't get him to donate a piece of *Lost* memorabilia to your favorite charity, and I sure as Shekels can't get him to go on your podcast...

In fact, if you want to invite me to go on your podcast, I'd better not find out after I have been on the podcast, and given you a piece of my soul, that the only reason you wanted me to be on your podcast was to see if you could become good enough podcast buddies with me to do you the favor of either calling Damon to be on your podcast, or giving you his digits so that you could call him and ask him to be on your podcast.

If it seems petty for me to bring this up, trust me, you have no idea the punishing frequency with which it happens.

Anyway, suffice it to say that around when Carlton joined us, Damon's mood was pitch black and exhausted. There was a very real possibility that *Lost* might have had to soldier on without its defining creative voice.

One afternoon, I was sitting in a colleague's office - we were working out some piece of scenework - when Damon entered to tell us that he was leaving, but that we should be fine in Carlton's capable hands. After much conversation, we said some confused and emotional good-byes and he left... and not just from that office... he quite literally walked out of the building and wasn't seen for the rest of the day... or the following day... or the day after!

As you might imagine, we were all pretty freaked out by this. I mean, we work in the rather sedate and corporate world of television for the luvva Jehovah: this was more like the music industry.

Another sign that made us wonder whether we would ever see Damon again, was, quite literally, a sign. While the placard in front of Damon's parking spot always read "EXECUTIVE PRODUCER DAMON LINDELOF," when the Disney facilities workers came in to attach a nameplate to Carlton Cuse's new parking spot, the sign read - I would later be told, at Damon's insistence - "SHOWRUNNER CARLTON CUSE."

What we soon learned was that Carlton had - very wisely, given Damon's level of fatigue - agreed to let him go for an unspecified amount of time to see if he would be able to relax and then return with a clearer head.

A week later, Damon came back from a retreat to the palm desert. No, people, he wasn't out wandering the wastes in sackcloth and confronting the devil, he had been at Two Bunch Palms - which you might remember as that nice spa featured in the Robert Altman film *The Player*. If he didn't look tanned, rested, and ready, Damon at least appeared willing to climb back into the ring with the now-confirmed-as-pop-culture-defining, massive-audience-gathering, monster hit that was *Lost*.

If anything seemed to convince Damon of how badly *Lost* needed him, it was probably hearing the story break developing on the whiteboard in his absence. Now, there had been times - and, again, I have heard him say as much in interviews -- when Damon expressed to us that he felt the show was literally sucking away his soul and that he wished he could jump. Sometimes he would even threaten to do it off a cliff...

However, when Damon Lindelof heard the beats to a story in which Hurley was revealed to be an amateur hypnotist who would use his abilities to pry to the location of the kidnapped Claire from the now-amnesiac Charlie, his pride of ownership came roaring back with bull force.

If ever there was a moment when I knew that there was no way Damon Lindelof would ever leave *Lost* again it was when he told us what he thought of that idea. (Eventually, hypnosis found its way into the show, in a second season episode in which tail section survivor Libby used it on Claire - I suppose that much of Damon's strenuous objections came from us giving that skill to Hurley.)

Over the years, Damon and Carlton came to be collectively known as "Darlton" by fans and chroniclers of the show. They were publicly acknowledged as the collective creative force behind *Lost* and were essentially inseparable, even going as far as to appear in bed together - like Bob Newhart and Suzanne Pleshette on the Newhart series finale - in a comedy sketch spoofing the *Lost* series finale on *The Jimmy Kimmel Show*.

The accomplishments of "Darlton" would be extraordinary. From our early success, "Darlton" created a way to sustain the show's pace of invention and novelty for years to come. They also became - among the likes of Shonda Rhimes, Joss Whedon, Matthew Weiner, and Kurt Sutter - the standard bearers of a new breed of rockstar showrunner whose celebrity is inextricable from the fame of their shows.

Most importantly, "Darlton" eventually negotiated the end date for the series: a move that relieved a great deal of tension from the creative process. Thanks to them, the writers of *Lost* - myself not included, as I was long gone by then - were able to set a creative goal and truly steer the ship there without the need for the sort of dramatic stalling of which we were so frequently, and occasionally accurately, accused.

Like everything else having to do with *Lost* - and, if you take nothing else from this lengthy read, life itself - "Darlton" did not appear *ex nihilo*. Even though Carlton had previously employed Damon, and Damon continued to consider him an Obi-Wan-like figure, this was a very different playing field: one in which Carlton's former mentee had an extraordinary amount of personal and emotional authorship and creative authority.

Carlton's immediate mandate would be to stabilize the creative matrix of the show, bring a stronger voice of command to the writers room, give Damon freedom from the managerial responsibilities of the series to focus on nailing down the show's creative concerns, provide collaborative support in making decisions about the direction of the series (a place where Damon often found himself pummeled by the massive amount of choices and conflicting opinions), and to insure the smooth, continuous delivery of material of equal quality to the first half of the season to our production in Hawaii.

Eventually "Darlton" would handle all of these duties collectively, and take together the bows for both the creative glory and the organizational efficiency of *Lost*. At the inception of this partnership, however, Carlton was first and foremost a seasoned manager who was there to support a less experienced one.

I was very flattered to be asked by Carlton to co-author his first script for the show, "Hearts and Minds." Carlton felt that I had a good bead on the voice of the series and that working with me would be helpful. Carlton must have been pleased with the result, because as new writers entered the show - first Leonard Dick, and then Eddy Kitsis and Adam Horowitz - Carlton would ask them to work with me, which is how I got to co-write "...In Translation" and "Born to Run."

Sadly, when I talk about "new writers entering the series," it is because some were asked to leave the series. As I said before, the *Lost* writers room was a contentious place and - while, in many shows, that spirit of debate is what makes the best ideas float to the surface - when that makes the show's creator feel like he has a parliament of adversaries waiting to undermine his vision, then changes have to be made.

The first thirteen episodes of a twenty-two-episode series are, essentially, a show's "shakedown" cruise. It is when the network orders a show's "back nine" that the first changes in the show's creative staff are made. Most contracts for writers and other creatives are split at the thirteenth episode, with an option to continue. The departures usually happen for the same reasons they do on any other job site: the personalities, styles, or vision of staff members don't jibe with those of the boss, or bosses in this case.

There's very little shame in being let go from a television show. It's an extremely common occurrence because the business is so nomadic and subjective, like "the show got cancelled" nomadic, and "you just don't get it" subjective. None of that makes firings any less traumatic, especially when the show on which you will no longer be working happens to be the biggest and most talked-about hit of the season.

As I said before, by the time the first season ended, every writer who began the season, other than me, was gone. When something like this happens, you are naturally beset by conflicting emotions.

You feel grateful to be asked back. You also feel shitty

for being the only one. You also feel bad because you spent more time in the past few months with these people than you did your own family and you have become very fond of them - not to mention that you feel that you built something truly special that would not be here without them. You also feel like you "get" why some of them didn't work out on the show.

Also, you get on with the show and keep earning your pay, you thank Jah these difficult decisions weren't yours to make, you hope that if you are next, your agent is busy leveraging the show's fame into a rich deal elsewhere... and after all the rupture, trauma, good-byes, and recriminations are done (one departing writer took me aside and accused me of "running a masterful political game" on our employers in order to secure my survival on the series), you mostly feel like that lyric from the Geto Boys... "When the fire dies down, what the fuck ya gonna do?"

As *Lost* entered its second season, we had run through a great deal of the backstory material we created in the think tank and through the first season. As a result of this expenditure, we had also established a world full of amazing characters who were ripe for further exploration. We had also agreed that in season two, we would mix things up by bringing in some new blood in the form of the tail section survivors... a plan we began to enact in season one through the radio transmission received by Boone, the ongoing mentions of Rose's husband Bernard, and, most saliently, the reveal of Ana-Lucia Cortez in the season finale.

More importantly, the success of the show made it possible to truly dig into our stash of ideas for revelations about the island. Because the think tank had been such a help in developing the show, it was decided that before we began to work on episodic ideas, the show's writing staff - which now comprised "Darlton," co-executive producers Steven Maeda, and Craig Wright, writer/producers Leonard Dick, Eddy Kitsis and Adam Horowitz working as a team, Elizabeth Sarnoff, and staff writer Christina Kim (assisted once again by Dawn and Matt, now joined by Gregg Nations, who would also go on to script coordinate for the remainder of the series as well as write) - would convene in a "minicamp" to decide which secrets would be revealed and when, and to chart the tentpoles for the season.

This would become the pattern for the rest of the seasons of *Lost*, the writers would meet to decide where the show was going that year, and then dig into weekly story, working from the broad strokes down to the individual episodes.

It was also during this minicamp that Craig Wright made his mark early by re-christening the Medusa Corporation as "The Dharma Initiative" and giving a name to its creator, Scandinavian billionaire and reformed weapons magnate Alvar Hanso. As things finally received the names they would have for years to come, they rose to the level of canon and prepared to take their place in the spotlight.

Another pattern that expressed itself during this first minicamp would become the *modus operandi* for the remainder of *Lost*. As Damon and Carlton solidified their preferred workflow and morphed into "Darlton" it quickly became clear that they would also take a heavier hand in the authorship of scripts. Rather than have individual writers shepherd their stories from the white-board through scripting, and then pre-production and on-set rewrites, "Darlton" would now have the room break stories and then team up writers to complete the scripts quickly, allowing them to more thoroughly re-evaluate the material on their own time.

From halfway through the first season, the practice of sending writer/producers to Hawaii to oversee production on their episodes was suspended to allow us to catch up on script and story generation and allow "Darlton" to make a stronger mark as the show's final word. With a show as complicated as *Lost*, this now became standard operating procedure: the writers were more needed in Burbank, plotting out the show's long arcs than on the set.

It also became standard practice for "Darlton" to peel away from the hubbub of the writers room to "work the show" on their own and then return to the room with fully-baked ideas for us to incorporate into arcs and stories.

Generally, I wouldn't find any of the above particularly disagreeable. Television is a collaborative medium, after all, and working at the pleasure of your showrunner - and in their preferred method, whatever that may be - is what we are paid to do. It is not the lot of me and my fellow hired guns to insist that the work tailor itself to us: it's the showrunner's world and you're just visiting, and we know that.

However, something about the application of these new workflows in the context of *Lost* changed my relationship with the show irrevocably.

Maybe I had too close an attachment to the romantic spirit of "brilliance from chaos" that characterized our first season, but I found all of this to be a comedown - and my relationship with both *Lost* and "Darlton" suffered. As season two progressed, I found myself more and more cut off from *Lost*'s creative mainstream, and it was hard to disguise my disaffection. (That much said, I've been told I suffer from "resting bitch face" so maybe that had something to do with it too.)

Even though I continued to play a key role in the development of series concepts such as the history of the Dharma Initiative (the first Dharma training film was part of "Orientation," which I co-wrote with Craig Wright), and much of my work during the second season involved fleshing out the Dharma Initiative's origins, discerning the meaning of the numbers, planting the Valenzetti Equation firmly in series canon, and creating a narrative for the work of the Hanso Foundation - both for the series and for a massive transmedia project called "The *Lost* Experience" - I was repeatedly told that my individual voice as a creator of story, character, and dialogue was becoming too idiosyncratic for the current direction of the show.

On February of 2006, I resigned.

It wasn't a huge dramatic moment, but rather an inevitable conclusion. We were still in the thick of our "first season victory lap," having already won the Emmy, TCA, and Golden Globe - and twenty-four hours after I resigned, I would be sharing the stage not just with "Darlton" but also all of the writers from the first season as well as all the current writers on the show.

Anyway, Damon and I chatted after work on a Friday night and agreed my time had come. I pitched the idea that I run my contract to the end of the season, continue to render services, work in the writers room, and shepherd "The *Lost* Experience" to completion. Frankly, I think we were all relieved to just have out in the open what everyone already knew: this founding member had become a square peg.

All that said, I loved *Lost* and never stopped fighting for it. "The *Lost* Experience" is a good example. Jordan Rosenberg - then a Disney Writing Fellow, now an accomplished writer whose credits include *Medium* and *Falling Skies* (not to mention my show *The Middleman*) as well as the Lost third season episode *"Par Avion"* - and I wrote every last word of that transmedia project, not only creating concepts that endured in the show's canon, but also taking on the task of making sure that everything we did passed muster with "Darlton" and ABC's promotion department.

At the same time we coordinated the production of the thing with our broadcast and online media partners in England and Australia - and managed such weird, out-of-the-box tasks as sourcing the production of candy bars, meeting with ad agencies to discuss such esoteric issues as whether or not we could integrate the creation of "lymon" into the work of the Hanso Foundation in order to forge a strategic partnership with Sprite, working with the editorial department of a major publishing house to put hints about the show in an otherwise unrelated novel, coordinating a global scavenger hunt, acting in (and improvising most of the content of) a series of fake radio broadcasts - and casting and producing dozens of web videos elaborating the story of the Dharma Initiative and its founders.

I participated in all of this through the summer of 2006, even though I was by then co-executive producer of the CBS/Paramount hit show *Medium*, and, most likely, rendering services to ABC in promotion of a show that aired on the same time slot was a flagrant breach of contract. Please tell no one.

On the day I cleaned out my office, the *Lost* writers

suite was deserted. The third season writers, including my replacement, had already been hired and the minicamp relocated to a resort in Hawaii.

I must admit that was a bitter pill... a resort in Hawaii sounded like a much better place to brainstorm than our offices in Burbank... and I did have some involvement in the success that paid for that trip. But, as I said before, the show must go on, and again, in the immortal words of the Geto Boys..."When the shit jumps off, what the fuck ya gonna do."

As I packed up two year's worth of stuff, a warm and welcome thought danced around my brain: an idea for *Lost*. As I had to write an email telling Damon that I would not be able to attend the screening he had planned for the season two finale (I only had one free week before starting on *Medium* and had planned a trip out of town), I added my idea to my regrets on the invitation and pledged that this would be the last thing I ever pitched him for *Lost*.

Hell, I was still on the payroll, so why not?

Damon responded warmly, and I went on my way... later, when the idea showed up in season three, I was ultimately gratified. Even on the last minute of the last day, I had been able to make a positive contribution to the future of something that had absolutely changed my life.

What was the idea?

Oh, come on. Do you think I learned nothing from JJ? I may be saying now that this is the last time I will speak publicly about *Lost*, but I would be a fool if I left nothing in the mystery box!

There are two stories that best reflect the joyous, life-changing side of having worked on something that, at least for a little while, changed the face of popular culture and influenced a worldwide audience...

While waiting to return home from a trip to France, I stood at a newsstand at Charles De Gaulle Airport. Turning to my wife, I said, "I bet I can pick out two magazines from this rack that have my picture in them." She took the dare.

I turned and plucked out a copy of the Official *Lost* Magazine, which was published worldwide, and one of the British Sci-Fi publications, *SFX*, where I had been interviewed that month because of my work on *Lost*. I was pictured in both.

If ever there was a more textbook case of having JUST the right amount of fame, that was it. Imagine being able to pull off that stunt, but not having so much fame that it decimates your privacy, inverts your moral priorities, causes you to lose all empathy for the rest of the world, and eventually drives you to a Britney Spearsian public downward spiral of substance abuse and head-shaving.

The second story takes place in my neighborhood dog park in the summer between seasons one and two.

This one man, a very soft-spoken and kind sort, would bring his sick dog - a once beautiful, now emaciated chocolate-colored pit bull terrier - to the park every morning. The dog was dying of canine leukemia, but the owner wanted him to spend his last days in the company of other dogs, and would let him play for as long as his frail body would allow.

One morning, we sat together on a bench, petting the bag of fur and protruding bones that had once been his strong and loyal companion. Tuckered out after just a little bit of light play, the dog slept fitfully at our feet, his visible ribs trembling with each passing breath.

With tears in his eyes, the man told me that his dog would probably be dead by the week's end. "He's a great dog," he said. "He's not just a great dog," I replied, "he has a great owner."

We wept together for a moment.

And then it got awkward.

I mean, aside from knowing each other's dogs, and a few cursory conversations - and this strange moment of shared emotional intimacy - we were kinda, sorta, well... total strangers.

So the man wiped his tears and asked me what I did for a living. I told him I was one of the writers of *Lost*.

His eyes saucered like a Tex Avery cartoon character. His voice went up a dozen decibels and at least one octave. Waving his hands into the air he exclaimed: "OH MY GAWD! CAN YOU TELL ME WHAT'S GOING ON IN THAT ISLAND?!?"

Ladies and gentlemen, the power of *Lost*.

Of course, none of this answers the one question, the only question that matters - the question that brought you here, Neo: "Did we know what we were doing, or were we just making it all up as we went?"

If you feel that I have not yet adequately addressed that... if you now consider yourself so strung along for so long that you are positively entitled to something brief and concise - something you can tell your friends at cocktail parties, something that accounts for the rigor of not just being entertained by six seasons of *Lost*, but also trudging through countless articles, and magazines, and documentaries, and clip shows, and making-of books, and "oral histories," and this rambling screed - OK, dear reader, here it is...

First we built a world. Then we filled it with an ensemble of flawed but interesting characters - people who were real to us, people with enough depth in their respective psyches to withstand years of careful dramatic analysis. Then we created a thrilling and undeniable set of circumstances in which these characters had to bond together and solve problems in interesting ways.

Soon thereafter, we created a way for you to witness their pasts and compare the people they once were with the people they were in the process of becoming. While that was going on, we also created an entire 747's worth of ideas, notions, fragments, complications, and concepts that would - if properly and thoughtfully mined - yield enough narrative fiction to last as long as our corporate overlords would demand to feed their need for profit and prestige, and then, just to be sure, teams of exceptionally talented people worked nonstop to make sure the 747 never emptied out.

And then we made it all up as we went.

THE AUDACITY OF BEING JADED

5.31.15

It's easy to believe that Hollywood is some sort of malignant entity whose job it is to turn the "good," "wholesome" and "deeply heartfelt" entertainments of our childhood into a physical graffito on our collective innocence.

I'd be lying if I didn't say that I often look at the billboards for the latest reinvention of something I once loved and take it as a personal affront... but as the years go by, and the entertainment/industrial complex goes predictably about the business of expectorating the necessary number of sequels, prequels, equals, reboots, remakes, and reduxes to keep the pumps primed and the money spigots open, I find myself reliving two pivotal moments in my relationship with my father - a man I not only adore, but also consider exceptionally wise.

In 1977, during one of my many fascinated, microscopic - and hyperverbal - explorations of the minutiae of *Star Wars* I noticed that my father, whom I had taken conversational hostage with that day's monologue (probably some speculation about Tusken Raider social dynamics and the ethics of making Banthas into beasts of burden), was slowly drifting away. Naturally, I immediately doubled down on my need for my father's attention and demanded to know how he could possibly be bored by something as shiny and awesome as *Star Wars*.

Starting, my father looked at me. As he processed my

question, his expression turned into a very amiable version of that much-imitated Robert DeNiro "shrug-sneer of resignation" - and said something to the effect of, "Well, you know, we had that." "Excuse me - you HAD that?"

My dad smiled, conveying to me that it just wasn't that new to him - what with his having grown up watching *Flash Gordon* movie serials and all.

My hair stood up on end. My eyes bugged out.

Flash Gordon? With the tin foil? And the visible wires holding up the dorky spaceships? And the gorilla-suited monsters, and the lame cardboard Hawkmen wings - and IN BLACK AND WHITE!?

FLASH GORDON?

The old man nodded - yeah, same thing, right?

Mercifully, this exchange didn't permanently damage my relationship with my father - but it did puzzle me for years. After that day, every time I made my parents take me to see the latest Amblin' flick, or the next two films in the original *Star Wars* trilogy, or the newest *Star Trek* sequel, I would look over to them and wonder what hopelessly primitive artifact of their childhood prevented them from fully enjoying the wonders on the screen.

About seventeen years ago, I started to hear about this thing called "*Harry Potter.*" Finally, when word of its wonders trickled down to me from people my own damned age, I broke down and bought the first book.

To me - and I know that even this will be seen as blasphemy by the faithful - *Harry Potter and the Sorcerer's Stone* was a delightful reinterpretation of the hero's journey with a dash of Fay Weldon and a pinch of the lighter side of Roald Dahl. Duly entertained, I pretty much left it at that, having no real desire to know anything else about Mr. Potter's future adventures - much less read six more increasingly door-stoppy tomes on the subject.

By the time Harry Potter became a seven-book, eight-movie-with-upcoming-spinoffs, theme park attraction, shared universe, global phenomenon that bridged the generation gap between Millennials, and Gens-X and -Y, I found myself sitting in the car with my 11-year-old niece... and having exhausted all of my ability to listen with rapt attention to her exegetic speculation on the manufacturing difficulties faced by the makers of "Bernie Bott's Every Flavor Beans" I drifted away into my own thoughts - and found myself the target of the same question I posed to my father decades before.

My answer was not dissimilar... "Well, you know, we had that."

The look of outrage on my niece's face remains etched in my memory to this day. Also, it's now on me that she will probably never read Fay Weldon in protest - which is a shame, because I have seldom had as great a ride with a novel as I did the first time I read *The Hearts and Lives of Men.*

My niece's newfound antipathy for Fay Weldon notwithstanding - and seriously, do yourself a favor and track down a copy of *The Lives and Loves of a She-Devil*, it will knock your socks off - the full reality of "Well, you know, we had that" didn't land on me until I watched the 2009 reboot of *Star Trek*.

Now, nü-*Star Trek* a very entertaining film... even though my entire takeaway is that it's the story of a pretty young man who is given a starship by a much older man as a reward for, well, little else than being pretty. (There may, indeed, be a great deal more pleasure to be had from re-watching nü-*Star Trek* as a sci-fi mutation of *Behind the Candelabra* with Christopher Pike as Liberace and James T.

Kirk as Scott Thorson, than as originally intended... but I digress.)

In any event, even as I enjoyed the many thrilling moments in this latest iteration of my beloved franchise, it quickly dawned on me that... well... for its many flaws - the ponderous pace and tone, the spackled on greasepaint make-up on all the leads, the disturbing tightness of the pajama-like duty uniforms, and the uncomfortable homoerotic subtext, just to name a few - I just plain LIKE Robert Wise's *Star Trek - The Motion Picture*.

A lot more.

Even if *Star Trek - The Motion Picture* - and subsequently *The Wrath of Khan* and *The Search for Spock* and their ilk - were about emotions profoundly out of the range of experience of a 12-year-old-boy (my age when I first saw that film in theaters), that primal experience of first experience can never be experienced again.

As fun as the 2009 nü-*Star Trek* reboot may have been, I'd already taken my first drink from that bottle thirty years earlier... and it doesn't matter that my vintage was a slow, and ponderous - and charmingly operatic - exploration of liberal white male menopause accompanied by visual effects that seem quaint to the modern eye.

For both better - and worse - that's what *Star Trek* means to me... ... and, well, you know, now I've had that.

None of this means I'm resigning from watching genre fiction and filmmaking, and not enjoying anything anymore, and tossing out all my James Blish novelizations in favor of the works of Thomas Mann (I'm a long way from committing to *The Magic Mountain* the same amount of time I've committed to *The Naked Time*).

I have, however, found in being jaded a certain liberation from, say, the outrage of reading that a beloved character may die in a future installment of a beloved franchise... or that an actor I dislike has been cast as my favorite hero... or the need to check out the latest trailer for some new version of a beloved property on fear of excommunication from the great guild of the over-informed, over-opinionated, and otaku-like.

Yes, the uniforms may be even shinier now... and yes, there's no visible matte lines on CGI model starships... and yes, no one under twenty will most likely understand what that last thing meant... but I've now been around the block. I now know the path of the hero's journey from beginning to end, and that means I don't have to start the journey from jump street each time - or jump at the chance to watch it retold endlessly.

Maybe the version of the hero's journey that is etched in my DNA is profoundly politically incorrect - or hopelessly stupid - I do come from an entire generation of men who think the archetypal James Bond is a pallid, and somewhat fey, older dandy who smiles during inappropriate moments and pervs out on unconscionably young women - but that's what I got when my pleasure receptors were ready to be influenced on a core level by such material...... and that opportunity only comes once.

Walking out of nü-*Star Trek,* I felt a certain wistfulness - like my season had passed.

No, it was a little harder than that.

It was like pop culture had just served me notice that I had conclusively aged out of the desired demographic target.

But the sting passed... quickly replaced by the memory of a conversation I'd had with my father two years earlier, when I phoned him from my car, upset that a friend had strong-armed me into going to see *Transformers 2.*

"Ah, yes... the *Revenge of the Fallen*," declared my father. "A GREAT film." "What are you talking about, Papi?" I replied. "Are you sure you heard me right?" "I did hear you right... and I have seen that film... in IMAX." "And you weren't horrified by the punishing length, the onslaught of cliched images, the frenetic ADD cutting, the horrible stereotypes, and the interminable action sequences?" "I did not look at the screen once," my father explained. "I spent my time in the theater turned away: watching the delighted faces of my grandchildren."

I took a moment, to process that, and then came back with another argument... "What about the oppressive soundscape, the cheese rock soundtrack, and the ear-shattering explosions?" "Ho... no, no, no," my father returned with a chuckle. "I wore earplugs."

THE TRANSMIGRATION OF GEORGE R.R. MARTIN

Originally Published in Uncanny Magazine, Issue #9
1.20.16, Revised 11.8.17

There's nothing out of the ordinary about a novelist becoming famous. There's also nothing new about the notion that eager audiences would follow the progress of a novelist whose work has become a sensation; or that the media would chronicle both the famous novelist's progress, and the exploits of the ardent fans. Hence that story we have all heard about American fans of Charles Dickens storming the port of New York for the delivery of the next chapter of *The Old Curiosity Shop*.

My favorite writer never experienced such acclaim in his time, although he occupies a strange place in The Pantheon as "The Novelist Who Has Had The Most of His Ideas Optioned For Films Without Anyone Actually Ever Making A Film That Actually Expresses His Actual World View In Any Actual Way." He is, of course, Philip K. Dick. I probably don't have to summarize his work, other than to say that he was obsessed with identity - personal, institutional, national, and spiritual - as a porous, shifting construct, and the ways in which technology usurps, replicates, and warps those identities.

Dick was also a master of telling these very high-concept stories that Hollywood has gobbled up like so many morsels of hallucinogenic candy (Precognitive cops! Secret agents who have been implanted with false memories! Reality is a virtual reality program to keep us from realizing that reality virtually sucks! The cops tasked to hunt down fake human beings are being policed by a false police department staffed by fake human beings!) from the point of view of downtrodden schlubs who just, really, want nothing more than to carve out a little bit of happiness only to find themselves utterly screwed over by technology... usually while being berated by a shrewish wife. One of the most fun things about introducing movie fans to Dick's work is watching the head-spins when they realize that Schwarzenegger in *Total Recall* is much closer to Woody Allen in the short story *We Can Remember it For You Wholesale*, or that Harrison Ford's brooding detective in *Blade Runner* is - in *Do Androids Dream of Electric Sheep* - a sad sack whose wife belittles him for his low income, and who can't to figure out the correct setting on his anti-depressant computer, or that John Anderton in *The Minority Report* is far closer to Dennis Franz than to Tom Cruise in *Minority Report*.

All of which brings me to the unique predicament of George R.R. Martin.

Though closer physically to Dennis Franz than Tom Cruise, Martin is far from a schlub: he turned from a lucrative career in TV to return to his first love, novel writing, in which he has accomplished great feats, including a return to television. That much said, Martin may be the first writer whose own life and work have come to encompass so vast a Möebius-loop of narratives, meta-narratives, and poly-narratives, that his very existence may be described as "Phildickian." Because the situation is ongoing, I am not sure that many appreciate the oddity of the man's predicament: those of us who care about Martin's work, and the increasingly labyrinthine story of its creation, are like the frog in a boiling pot of narrative convolution.

Whether or not Martin intended his seven-volume epic *A Song of Ice and Fire* to be his *magnum opus* and the song of his soul is moot. Most expect this to be Martin's last stand; an idea that seems validated by his age and the pace of his writing. As *magna opera* go, one would be hard pressed to beat *A Song of Ice and Fire,* and if it is not, indeed, the song of Martin's soul, it at least is the grand summation of its creator's ability and worldview. A few books into Martin's saga, the books were turned into the HBO show *Game of Thrones*. The series is insanely successful: the first fantasy show - arguably the first pure genre show - to win a best drama Emmy, and a phenomenon chronicled slavishly by the entertainment-journalism-industrial-complex[2].

As the pace of TV production quickly lapped Martin's ability to execute his vision in prose, the writer/producers - both in collusion with, and occasionally in spite of, him - have had to make up their own version of Martin's story using signposts Martin has described but not fleshed out in his novels, and about which he may still change his mind as he goes about the task of crafting his version of the story. As the popularly reported narrative has it, George R.R. Martin is, essentially racing - and losing to - a team of writers, producers, actors, and directors (which include himself), to complete a vast narrative tapestry which he has not completely figured out, but which is essentially the summation of his own artistic life... and perhaps the song of his soul.

This brings up a host of Phildickian questions: "Which

---

2   Though the series adaptation of *The Man in the High Castle* currently streaming on Amazon may just blow that title out of the water.

of the two, (novels or TV series) is the 'real' *Song of Ice and Fire*?" Is the television version of Martin's work even an adaptation once it moves past Martin's own conception of the events of his novels (a mathematical analysis of Martin's output has him completing the seventh book in 2023, by which time the television series will long have been completed)? Can Martin's own concept of the novels survive untainted by the narrative that will be developed once the team of writers which includes him beats him to the finish line?

Because of the popularity of Martin's work, Martin's own life has also become the subject of an increasingly polarized (and polarizing) meta-narrative that could easily be called *A Song of What George R.R. Martin is Doing Other Than Writing His Books*. As a modern celebrity, Martin is ubiquitous, but the longer it takes for him to finish his books, the more that the media's coverage of his life takes on the sheen of evidence-gathering for both sides for a Netflix documentary about an upcoming trial for the crime of disappointing his readers.

Though we are not used to seeing such things as interviews, feature stories, behind-the-scenes electronic press kits, news reports, blogs, and mainstream and academic criticism or even highfalutin' think pieces as part of the fiction of entertainment, they are every bit as constructed and "storified" for your enjoyment. The cultural footprint of a project as popular as *A Song of Ice and Fire* spawns a vast ecosystem of intertwined narratives, all designed to be as compelling as the flagship series. The more sophisticated the media at the disposal not just of the press, but of civilian bloggers, critics, twitterers, and so on, the greater, more varied, and less controlled by the commercial interests of the publishers/networks - and therefore more interesting - the cloud of narrative becomes.

Writing novels - especially longitudinal sagas with hundreds of character in dozens of interconnected plot-lines set in an entirely made-up universe - is a deeply personal process... but Martin is now working like Harlan Ellison in those store windows - only that window looks out into an entire industry based around chronicling his every keystroke and extrapolating how it may affect his production of the saga. Even the most unconcerned of consumers seems to know that Martin works on an old DOS machine, that he takes time off to watch the NFL, and that his heavy schedule of convention appearances cuts into his writing time. Martin himself has become a popular talk show guest, has appeared in comedy sketches lampooning both his magnum opus (the Conan O'Brien "Saturday morning cartoon *Game of Thrones*" in which Martin signs off by cheerfully declaring "*Valar Morghulis*, kids!") and the reported pace of his writing (Martin appeared as "Zombie George R.R. Martin" in the apocalyptic drama *Z Nation*: signing copies of "A Dream of Spring," the last novel of *A Song of Ice and Fire*, long after the end of civilization as we know it).

As the guest appearances, self-portrayals, interviews, news reports, blogs, counter blogs, and tweets pile up, one might ask "will the real George R.R. Martin please stand up?" Is he a jolly professional talk show guest? A deadbeat creator so intoxicated by fame that he takes long stretches off the keyboard to command fans to bring him cheese burgers to his room at conventions? Is he a thoughtful and deeply artistic soul forced to endlessly explain the artistic process to the detriment of said process? Is he a once-great NFL blogger whose novel writing sideline now cuts deeply into his true love of the gridiron?

Is the person known to the world as "George R.R. Martin" (the protagonist of *The Song of the Making of A Song of Ice and Fire*) even anything like the real man?

In truth, George R.R. Martin is probably all those things, and none, and many more. I'd even guess that as a person, he's probably pretty comfortable in the spectrum of his own consciousness and doesn't see himself as a bundle of idealized, stereotypical *dramatis personae* - or the victim of a Phildickian identity crisis.

Audiences, however - even ones that watch *Game of Thrones* - are used to protagonists having singular goals in a tightly defined moral space. As a character in an ongoing global, community-generated dramatic narrative of creation, most people need "George R.R. Martin" to be one thing: hero, villain, deadbeat, Falstaffian victim of fame, etc. Being a "real person" however, makes Martin unpredictable and, as a result, there's multiple "George R.R. Martins" to serve all narrative needs. As an audience we are stuck with "George R.R. Martin" as the lead of *The Song of the Making of A Song of Ice and Fire,* regardless of how "confusing" his behavior might be - and his identities are many depending on the chronicler, medium, and agenda.

One of the more interesting words to emerge from the confluence of narrative and technology is "transmedia": coined by then-MIT Professor Henry Jenkins to describe stories told across multiple platforms in which the totality cannot be understood unless the reader has fluency in a variety of storytelling modalities. To me, *The Song of the Making of A Song of Ice and Fire* is the first true transmedia story in that, rather than a narrative scavenger hunt that is still directed through something somewhat resembling authorial intent, it is being generated in real time, by many people, over many years, and no one - not even the author of the core work - knows the real end.

The most interesting question here isn't even "Will Martin finish his work?" or "Which of the two simultaneously-generated versions is the best - or most authentic - depiction of a fictional land that once was the unique domain of its creator's mind?" or even "Will the real Westeros / George R. R. Martin / *Game of Thrones/Song of Ice and Fire* please stand up?" Rather, I ask myself "how does a creator stay pure to a vision of himself and his work when his life and creation are themselves the subject of a meta-narrative of such unprecedented density over so many genres and media?"

All of which brings me back to Philip K. Dick. My favorite interpretation of a Phildickian thought experiment lies in a commonly articulated answer to the eponymous question of his novel *Do Androids Dream of Electric Sheep?* To many the answer is that it doesn't matter, what matters is that they dream. Which leads me to wonder if it matters whether George R.R. Martin and his creative process have been in any way changed or informed by all of this attention.

Perhaps what matters is that, in telling his story, Martin has become the center of a much larger story that will hover over him and his creation long after the novels are complete and consigned to the page. Anyone who reads the full text of *A Song of Ice and Fire* once Martin has completed it - and for as long as the Internet exists - will be able to dive into a true rabbit hole of controversy and meta-narrative with the click of a few buttons. That rabbit hole is, and will be, by itself a narrative experience that will be unique to any person because no two readers will experience it in the same order... and perhaps that is the truth of all narrative in the post-modern era: the blockbuster novel, the tentpole film, the best-selling novel - are they objects with their own integrity or are they inseparable from the inevitable pageant of commercial, journalistic, and critic- and fan-driven response for their narrative resonance?

Hopefully by the time these questions are answered, both George R.R. Martin and "George R.R. Martin," whoever they may be, will be sitting somewhere comfortable, enjoying a well-deserved rest, and watching the game.

FORTY-SIX TWEETS ABOUT ANTHONY BOURDAIN'S SUICIDE

6.8.18

i am working to divest myself from social media because, after many years, i became concerned that courting the good graces of others was becoming more important to me than my own knowledge of myself. (1/46)

(or, as i recently told a friend "social media is really messing with the purity of my narcissism") (2/46)

for that reason, i am reticent to speak on a hot button issue. many are already adding their two cents. some with no reason other than to call attention to themselves. i really don't care for that in others or myself. (3/46)

nevertheless, i want to put this out there in the hopes that it helps someone either understand or feel understood. (4/46)

during my young and adult life, there has not been a single day that i have not - at least once in my waking hours - seriously considered suicide. (5/46)

this should not be surprising. i am a diagnosed depressive who takes medication daily and visits a psychotherapist weekly. i also work in an industry that is notorious for madness, rage, and abuse. (6/46) it is also neither a source of pride, nor a revelation i am making in hopes of triggering an intervention or outpouring of any sort... and it sure as shit doesn't make me "special". (7/46)

this is merely a truth of my life: one of the ongoing, and overwhelming, themes of my existence is that i hate myself and want to die. (8/46)

i have planned and rehearsed my own death with depressing regularity. after forty plus years, the comings and goings of these thoughts are as rote as brushing my teeth. (9/46)

though at different times - and currently - the medications and therapy have reduced this sometimes overwhelming noise to a background hum, it nevertheless remains. constant. waiting. (10/46)

in therapy, i have often hoped for a weepy, cathartic epiphany to match some dramatic arc of healing, perhaps leading to a permanent banishment of the black dog. (11/46)

the truth is far less glamorous. the black dog abides. (12/46)

what i've learned to do over decades is to manage the severity of - and co-exist with - my depression and all of the thoughts of self-annihilation that it brings. (13/46)

every day the thoughts arrive. most days i drive them back to where they came from. on the days they attack with force and purpose, all i can do is buy myself time until the storm breaks... (14/46) or at least until i am back on my therapist's couch. or until something forces me out of my frame of reference. (15/46)

in four decades i have gotten very good at buying time for myself. (16/46)

recently, the thought of my wife and daughter have become the best way to do this - along with the reminder that i know the love of proud and caring parents. (17/46)

occasionally, the purchase has to be made with bleaker coin. (18/46)

there are days when the fear of botching the job and not just being maimed, but having to go through the tedium of listening to others gently assuring me of the value of living - while maimed - is enough. (19/46)

some days, engagement with meaningful hard work does the trick. (20/46)

some days, you ask for help. that doesn't mean hysterical midnight phone calls: sometimes, when you simply schedule a lunch date, the binding social commitment to show up somewhere is all it takes to frustrate the black dog. (21/46)

as anyone who has done suicide hotline work will tell you, extracting a promise of a near-future appearance can be a useful tool in forcing a suicidal person to look past a moment of despair. (22/46)

some days, you just focus on the task of breathing... on accomplishing the minimum requirements for the - at times seemingly sisyphean task - that is moving through each recurring moment of life. (23/46)

some days, i just set the words "i hate myself and i want to die" to music. (24/46)

though it has too many syllables, i have learned that i can do a reasonable job of shoving it into the melody of "i hate myself for loving you." (25/46)

between all those things - and the therapeutic intervention of caring professionals - it is absolutely possible to cobble together a happy, successful, thriving life. (26/46)

i have one of those. i know it. i am grateful. it doesn't change the basic reality. the black dog abides. (27/46)

to me, "perspective" means carving out a space where the black dog exists alongside everything else that makes me and has no greater or lesser importance. (28/46)

none of us is any more the sum of our damage than we are the sum of our successes. we are each all of it... (29/46)

and we each have to find a way to let these things - both positive and negative - find their level without destroying us. (30/46)

for me - and i have to believe others like me - every day is a dark field strewn with match boxes. some days, the light is within easy reach... (31/46)

others are a protracted, exasperating grope that makes one wonder if the supply has finally run out. then i buy time and eventually discover the matchbox was at my feet the whole time. (32/46) when i heard that a prominent person who, by all accounts, was truly decent and good, did himself in at the age of 61, i had some of the same sad and mournful thoughts that many have expressed. (33/46)

but i also thought "he lasted sixty one years, choosing every day to live, do meaningful work, and spread a positive message of inclusivity, learning, and hospitality." (34/46)

gallows as that may sound - and inasmuch as i can extrapolate another person's struggles from my own - anyone who fights off the dog that long and manages to accomplish so much deserves a medal.(35/46)

if there is a heaven, st. peter is no doubt welcoming the man with open arms and offering him the clicker. (36/46)

if you protest a suicide with rage at the victim's "cowardice", you are entitled to your opinion... but know this, to the depressed, you are every bit as alien as we are to you. (37/46)

some of us truly can not understand how "normal" people open their eyes in the morning without thinking "oh shit, not again". (38/46)

living is a choice for some - and making that choice day in and day out signifies an inner strength that i have learned to respect. (39/46)

ernest hemingway famously said that "the world breaks everyone". i take that as gospel, and feel deeply for anyone for whom that breaking force begins at the source of their own soul. (40/46) every time i visit a psychiatrist, i am told new drugs are "in the pipeline" which will cause the dramatic healing that eons of narrative storytelling have deceived us into believing is possible. (41/46)

until then, know that for many, suicide is a viable option to both ease the pain of living, and satisfy a self-loathing so pervasive that it demands nothing less than annihilation. (42/46)

if you do not have to choose life daily, good for you. you have other choices. you can choose to exercise compassion. you can choose to practice kindness. you can choose to refrain from judgment. (43/46)

you can also choose not to put whatever shit-wit first thought comes to mind on social media because you have been beguiled into thinking that the dopamine rush of being "liked" by a few strangers is equal to actual accomplishment. (44/46)

mostly, you can choose to understand those unlike you: and take the risk that, if you dedicate a little time to studying what you don't know, you may wind up only learning how little you know... (45/46)

and if the thought of something like that humbling you into silence frightens you, then learn what some of us learn anew every day: hard choices are worth making. (46/46)

IN PRAISE OF *DEUS* (EX MACHINA)

Originally Published In Uncanny Magazine, Issue #16
3.12.17

The fourth episode of the seventh season of the CBS sit-com *The Big Bang Theory* - titled "The Raiders Minimization" - has apparently become a classic. I say "apparently" because, though I am not a habitual watcher, I have become keenly aware of this half hour of television by dint of being dragged into the same discussion about it several times, in several writers rooms, over the course of the last few years.

I suppose that - in a workplace where narrative construction is the life and limb, and where so many of us revere Lucas and Spielberg, and where *Raiders of the Lost Ark* is considered holy scripture - it is inevitable that some contrarian will bring up the following scene as proof that they understand a storytelling sleight-of-hand that continues to elude both the general public and the rank-and-file of dramatic storytellers:

AMY: It was very entertaining
despite the glaring story problem.

SHELDON: Story problem? You, oh,
Amy, what a dewy-eyed moon-calf you
are. **Raiders of the Lost Ark** is
the love child of Steven Spielberg
and George Lucas, two of the most

```
gifted filmmakers of our generation.
I've watched it 36 times, except
for the snake scene and the face-
melting scene, which I can only
watch when it's still light out,
but, I defy you to find a story
problem. Here's my jaw, drop it.

AMY: All right. Indiana Jones plays
no role in the outcome of the
story. If he weren't in the film, it
would turn out exactly the same.

SHELDON: Oh, I see your confusion.
You don't understand. Indiana Jones
was the one in the hat with the
whip.

AMY: No, I do, and if he weren't
in the movie, the Nazis would have
still found the Ark, taken it to
the island, opened it up and all
died, just like they did... (Off
his dropped jaw) Let me close that
for you.
```

Debunking the premise that the sum of Indiana Jones's actions in *Raiders of the Lost Ark* somehow amounts to a null narrative outcome and therefore makes up a "story problem" is easy - and, frankly, academic - so let's get that out of the way first...

Raiders - and its prequel *Indiana Jones and the Temple of Doom,* and sequels *Indiana Jones and the Last Crusade* and *Indiana Jones and the Kingdom of the Crystal Skull* - all teach roughly the same moral virtue: letting go of material desire is necessary for spiritual enlightenment... - In *Temple of Doom*, a younger, and significantly cockier, Indiana Jones trades his stated desire for "fortune and glory" for faith in the lost Sankara stone. - In *Last Crusade*, Indy and his father see their fractious relationship conclusively healed as Henry Jones Senior absolves Junior from the belief that he must acquire the Holy Grail in order to finally make him proud. - Finally, in *Kingdom of the Crystal Skull*, Indiana Jones sees all his opponents vanquished because they do not realize that the true treasure of the trans-dimensional aliens who built the titular citadel was the knowledge they gained by visiting our world, not the riches they hoarded in their stronghold.

Though somewhat chastened from his lust for "fortune and glory" by the events of its prequel, Indiana Jones enters *Raiders of the Lost Ark* as a driven and ruthless treasure hunter for whom acquisition of academically significant relics before any of his many competitors - and all of the associated discoveries - is the only goal. Jones casually blasphemes God and the Ark more frequently than the Nazis he opposes, and his arch-nemesis - the oily French mercenary René Belloq - clearly respects the divine power of the Ark with far greater piety than does our hero.

After suffering an enormous amount of peril and loss - forsaking everything to protect the Ark, even if it means letting the Nazis have it - Indiana Jones finally gets the chance to stare at the face of God... and what does he do?

He realizes that he is unworthy.

Then - with a humility more powerful than the many feats of strength and endurance he has performed through the story - Indiana Jones saves himself and his girlfriend by turning away from the very treasure he has sought the

entire film. For those of you who have not seen *Raiders*,
God then shows up and smites Belloq and the Nazis
with a display of light and magic that can only be called
"industrial". After all the smoke and carnage clears, only
Indiana Jones and Marion Ravenwood remain, having
borne (not) witness to the wrath of the Divine.

The argument that Indiana Jones' failure to prevent
the Nazis from getting the Ark is a deep narrative flaw
only makes sense if you ignore what *Raiders of the Lost Ark*
is actually about; a knight errant who earns the ultimate
"gimme" from a wrathful God. Indiana Jones' character
arc is that - of all the eponymous "Raiders" - he alone is the
one that comes to an understanding that the film's titular
action is morally wrong.

From jump street, it is made clear that preventing
the greatest villains in history from getting the greatest
weapon in eternity is among the lesser of Indiana Jones'
motivations. Jones doesn't even seem afraid that he is
about to tamper with powers beyond the scope of human
imagination, as he responds to his best friend and mentor's
warnings of the Ark and its secrets: "Marcus, what are
you trying to do, scare me? You sound like my mother. I'm
going after a find of incredible historical significance and
you're talking about the boogeyman."

By the end of the film, Jones' facile faithlessness in the
face of academic achievement is wiped away clean - along
with any other corollary motivations - by the revelation
that good and evil are equally powerless before the face
of an omnipotent God... and that God spares those who
sacrifice their self-interest in service of what is right.

In this way, *Raiders of the Lost Ark* is an anomaly in
tent-pole filmmaking and a direct subversion of the myth
of the American matinee idol. American matinee idols all

have one thing in common: they NEVER quit... and yet the natural endpoint of Indiana Jones' quest is that he learns <u>when</u> to quit. In doing so, Indiana Jones finally achieves grace, earns love, and - yes - defeats the Nazis.

Imagine that. An American matinee hero saving the day by doing <u>nothing</u>.

It is a testament to the nascent stage of the American blockbuster film in 1979 to 1981 - when *Raiders* was conceived, filmed, and released - and the combined clout of its director, producer, and writers, that they were able to get away with this ending. I certainly cannot imagine it happening today, when movies are cogs in franchise machines concocted by "story groups" and in which a film of similar scale has to satisfy and monetize audiences both foreign and domestic in order to achieve its sales projections.

Of course, it is unfair to expect that a mainstream four-camera sitcom like *The Big Bang Theory* would reflect the reality of geek culture with Frederick Wiseman-like fidelity. It makes sense that - for the sake of comedy - *Big Bang* would take the low-hanging fruit of a treasured film featuring a literal *Deus Ex Machina* for a take-off point for a story about geeks "ruining" beloved properties for one another.

That being as it may, *Raiders of the Lost Ark* is far from an incompetent work of seat-of-the-pants improv, but rather a considered, calculated work by four master filmmakers at the prime of their craft. In 1979, you would have been hard-pressed to name a better "dream team" for popcorn entertainment than Steven Spielberg, George Lucas, Lawrence Kasdan, and Philip Kaufman. Though not infallible, these men were not careless, which is why *Raiders* remains a classic of the mainstream Hollywood cinema to this day.

All of this begs the question: does *Raiders of the Lost Ark* truly NEED so full-throated a defense against the perceived depredations of *The Big Bang Theory*?

The answer is, of course "no" ... even though many professional writers - and even just fanboys - have taken the show's pop-comedic analysis of *Raiders* to heart as if it were meaningful. There is, however, a vital weapon in every writer's armamentarium, that does need a full-throated defense and reevaluation.

I am, of course, talking about the *Deus Ex Machina*.

Long the *Bête Noir* of high school and college creative writing teachers across the land, every writer has a story of having it drilled into her or his skull that a *Deus Ex* is nothing less than admission of narrative failure. Everyone who ever sat through a regional production of one of Moliere's farces for a literature class has a memory of the speech that followed from the teacher: that the *Deus Ex* at the end of said farce was a common narrative device back in the "olden times," but that we - who benefit from hindsight and modernity - are above such trickery, and that no honest writer working today would even DARE try such a thing.

Because the *Deus Ex Machina* has fallen so far out of narrative fashion as to become a modern shibboleth for "lazy writing" - which is the reason I suspect so many of my peers have embraced "The Raiders Minimization" as a sort of "gotcha!" - I find it especially curious that several of the most formative films of my childhood all rely on the device for their narrative resolution... and that all of them were released in 1981... and that all of them were financially successful in their time and remain respected works of the popular arts to this day.

The first is, of course, *Raiders of the Lost Ark* - the top grossing film of 1981. Then there's the third highest-grossing film of 1981, *Superman II* (in which Superman is given back his powers by his god-like father after losing them for favoring the love of Lois Lane over his duties as protector of humanity).

Rounding up the list are the tenth highest-grossing film of 1981, Terry Gilliam's *Time Bandits*, and the eighteenth highest-grossing film of 1981, John Boorman's Wagnerian retelling of Arthurian legend, *Excalibur* (in which both King and Land are restored to greatness after being served a drink from the Holy Grail by one of his long-suffering quest knights).

One could even argue that 1981 was some sort of golden age/last gasp of the *Deus Ex Machina* in popular film... especially since 1982 is considered by many genre fans and film scholars as the year that the tentpole blockbuster came into its modern form with the summer releases of *E.T.: The Extra Terrestrial, Poltergeist, Star Trek II: The Wrath of Khan, Conan The Barbarian, 48 Hours, The Road Warrior, The Thing, Blade Runner,* and *Rocky 3.* All of these were commercially successful mass entertainments, all are generally considered to be quality films, and they are understood to have set the pattern for high-earning summer films to this day.

Also, most of these films were either written, directed, or acted in by talent that continues to do similar work to commercial success today (Steven Spielberg, Ridley Scott, George Miller, Sylvester Stallone, Arnold Schwarzenegger, Harrison Ford, Eddie Murphy, Kurt Russell) or represent franchises that still hover near the top of the mass entertainment heap (*Star Trek, Mad Max, Rocky, Blade Runner*).

Was 1981 the final year in which *Deus Ex* was acceptable as a narrative trope in pop culture? Was 1982 the year in which mainstream entertainment was taken over by an anti-*Deus Ex* generation that would banish it for decades to come? Did a cabal of Hollywood's new and elite vanguard of commercial mainstream filmmakers meet in a dark and smoke-filled room in the back of some old-timey Hollywood haunt after 1981 and decide that - for the sake of modernity, profit, and the appeasement of creative writing teachers across the land - the *Deus Ex* was to be staked through the heart for the betterment of commercial entertainment?

The truth is, as with all things, far less glamorous.

It's not as if the directors of the *Deus Exes* of 1981 went into creative exile: John Boorman continued his artistically successful career well after 1981. Terry Gilliam's greatest Hollywood successes were still a decade away. Richard Donner - who, while not the director of record, originated *Superman 2*, directed more than half of the final product, and oversaw the development of the script with Tom Mankiewicz - would soon unleash the *Lethal Weapon* series, which became a hardy perennial of the summer multiplex, and also direct that most beloved of Gen-Y pop-cultural artifacts, *The Goonies*.

Of course, none of these films would feature the *Deus Ex;* Martin Riggs' capacity to survive beatings that would macerate ordinary men notwithstanding.

To fully understand why *Deus Ex Machina* - both in the farcical and completely-out-of-left-field sort so loathed by writing teachers, and in the wholly-earned and artistically-warranted form seen in *Raiders of the Lost Ark* - just plain <u>feels</u> so wrong... one need only look at 1981's most egregious deployer of the tactic: Terry Gilliam in *Time*

Bandits.

Time Bandits is possibly the darkest, most subversive, anti-establishment movie to appear in a top ten highest-grossing film list in the last forty years: a sin for which it is now mostly-forgotten, and - most tellingly - thoroughly un-remade and un-rebooted. It may also be my favorite film of my childhood... with *Raiders of the Lost Ark* very close in the mix.

In telling the story of a curious boy who finds a time portal in his bedroom - and embarks on an adventure with six thoroughly amoral dwarves who have stolen a map of time portals from God himself, and plan to use it to steal every ancient treasure imaginable - *Time Bandits* claims a spiritual kinship to the gruesome, brutal original stories of the Brothers Grimm by way of *Monty Python's Flying Circus* (of which Gilliam is a member).

The single overwhelming message of *Time Bandits* is that the lives of adults consist of a worthless struggle to mitigate the absurdity of existence - and the loss of imagination and wonder concomitant with adulthood - though wanton violence, the toxic and arbitrary exercise of authority, and predatory consumerism.

In every one of the Bandits' adventures - whether meeting historical figures like Napoleon, or mythical ones like Robin Hood - adults are venal, stupid, infantile, and consumed with ego to the diminishment of all involved. The only creature of reason in *Time Bandits* is the boy at its center: Kevin. But even his plaints that the Bandits should go after knowledge instead of money fall on deaf ears as he and the Bandits traverse one historical vignette after another in search of filthy lucre.

Only one grown-up in the story survives Gilliam's scorn, and that is King Agamemnon (played by Sean

Connery). Of course, after emerging as a heroic, caring, and idealized adoptive father figure for Kevin, the Time Bandits emerge through a time portal to steal the boy back before he is able to settle into a worthy life of purpose with a loving parent.

Ripped from the one place where he might have been happy, Kevin and the Bandits ultimately find themselves in pitched battle against God's arch-nemesis: the Evil Genius. Consumed with the desire to use God's map to remake creation as a sort of consumerist technocracy, Evil Genius lures the Bandits to his Fortress of Ultimate Darkness with the temptation of riches beyond compare.

In the film's climax, the Bandits appear to abandon Kevin to be killed by Evil Genius, only to reappear with reinforcements culled from history: an army of Greek archers, a posse of gunslingers, a cavalry of medieval jousters, a World War Two tank, and a laser-cannon-equipped starship. It is a stirring moment of redemption for the otherwise horrible dwarves, who - having finally learned a lesson or two about the value of friendship - show up to defend their comrade and save creation.

Being a technocrat, Evil Genius easily wrests control of the weapons from our heroes and proceeds to spectacularly hand them their asses... but just as he is about to slaughter them all, God himself manifests on the scene (in the doddering form of a superannuated, three-piece-suit-wearing Sir Ralph Richardson) and rewards the plucky dwarves for their character pivot by smiting Evil Genius into a pillar of carbon.

Unconvincingly declaring that the theft of the map by the Bandits - and all the attendant mayhem they have caused - were part of his plan all along, God gathers up his property, along with most of the remains of Evil Genius, and the Bandits, and returns with them all to "Creation". Kevin is left behind to awaken in his bedroom to a fate that may be the single most depressing confirmation of the essential loneliness of humanity in the history of the mainstream cinema.

It is hard to imagine a film with the plot and theme I just described being made as popular entertainment, much less it cracking the year-end top-ten box-office list. *Time Bandits* is not only profoundly weird, it is also profoundly angry, and willing to end on an extreme note of such existential discomfort that it is difficult to imagine it being marketed to children.

Though their dramatic resolutions are similar - unsavory protagonists finally stick up for what is right in the face of insurmountable odds and receive a blessing from an inscrutable deity - *Raiders* did such a good job of convincing everyone that its intimate story of a single man's spiritual redemption was, in fact, the beginning of a billion-dollar franchise of movie serial-inspired derring-do, that the "discovery" of its *Deus Ex Machina* has become fodder for sitcoms and writing professional one-upmanship.

Similarly, audiences that love *Superman II* are comfortable accepting a Kryptonian patriarch's power mulligan because Superman is a. neither the newest nor the least subtle Christ metaphor out there, and b. an homage to immigrants who come to our country to use their foreign ways to fight for Truth, Justice, and the American Way, and he needed to get out of his predicament to kick Zod, Ursa, and Non out of the White House. Most people may make the argument that *Superman II* is "cheesy," but they seldom use it as an example of the dreaded *Deus Ex*.

Finally, Arthurian myth has had the Grail baked into its DNA over centuries. The inclusion of a last-minute healing of King Arthur by the Cup of Christ was not exactly a surprise in a film like *Excalibur*, which sought to synthesize the totality of Arthurian lore into one convenient mythopoetic package.

Time Bandits, however, offers no such comfort. As a shadowy reflection of *Raiders* in the Great Fraternal Hall of the Wholly-Earned and Dramatically-Valid *Deus Ex*, Gilliam's film lays bare the subversive nature of Spielberg and company's work by clarifying beyond the shadow of a doubt that the wholly-earned and dramatically-valid *Deus Ex Machina* is nevertheless a thoroughly depressing prospect.

After all, by the time the Nazis have the power to move thousands of men into Egypt like an invading army and excavate the city of Tanis, there is little a single man could possibly do to stop them... even when that single man is both a formidable intellectual and bullwhip brawler with an inexhaustible hunger for academic accomplishment.

The human cost of defeating the Third Reich is known to anyone with a rudimentary education: no one goes into *Raiders of the Lost Ark* thinking that the film will suddenly become an alternate history by either letting the Bad Guys get a hold of the most powerful weapon ever discovered, or letting the Good Guys get it in time to stop the coming war. The sad truth is that, in the end, Indiana Jones was destined to fail in every respect other than self-improvement.

Similarly, as Kevin is left behind in the denouement of *Time Bandits*, God answers the Bandits' question of whether their new friend can come along with them to the hereafter with a line that would have made Albert Camus proud: "Oh, don't go on about it... he's got to stay here to carry on the fight."

Of course Indiana Jones stayed in the popular culture to carry on the fight: learning the same lesson over and over again like some amnesiac archaeological Sisyphus... and Kevin ends Time Bandits standing over the smoldering ruins of what was once his home - with his parents literally blown to smithereens by a fragment of the Evil Genius that God somehow forgot to gather up in his haste - alone, and destined to "carry on the fight" forever in the faceless suburban sprawl from whence he came.

So the reason for the disappearance of the Deus Ex in popular culture makes complete sense not just as the triumph of a thousand educators, but as a triumph of commerce. Who wants to go to a summer movie to learn that the Nazis can't be beaten by a single matinee idol? Who wants to be told in a movie about a boy and his time traveling dwarves that existence is absurd and meaningless, adult pursuits are based on bad faith and delusion, and God is a doddering incompetent?

And yet, out of the Indiana Jones oeuvre, *Raiders* is universally understood - by a wide margin - as the best, most artistically successful, and dramatically rich of the quartet.

And yet, when I saw *Time Bandits* at age eleven - a time when I was beginning to realize just how misfit I felt in the world - I took from it not just a mind-bending, reality-warping sense of existential discomfort... but also the seemingly contradictory validation that other people saw the world through the same lens of fear, depression, and bewilderment that I did.

Time Bandits made me feel like my tribe was out there. *Time Bandits* left me depressed as a story, but hopeful as a human being.

Similarly, the end of *Raiders of the Lost Ark* was a revelation to me - and a statement of mature artistic thinking far greater than any of Spielberg and company's later attempts at "serious" cinema - precisely because it coexists with the same tropes it undermines. The end of *Raiders* is an admission that the world is so varied and strange - and so resistant to the monoliths we believe so unconquerable - that the contradictory archetypes of the heroic matinee idol and the *Deus Ex* can simultaneously occupy the same space, but only if your mind is wide enough open.

Sure, Spielberg went on to win all the Oscars for high-minded, "adult" films like *Schindler's List, Saving Private Ryan, Lincoln, The Color Purple,* and *Munich*... but none of those later - and to my mind leaden - efforts at enlightening his audience to such grown-up concepts as "man's inhumanity to man" compare in my book to the crazy wisdom on display at the conclusion of Indiana Jones' first cinematic adventure.

Now that I see *Raiders* through the lens of Indiana Jones' character arc (as opposed to merely basking in it as an example of impeccably choreographed action and the exultation of filmmaking and pulp fiction so clearly on display) I know that even my idols - the great filmic wizards whose fantasies inspired me as a child - were, at one point, able to see the absurd comedy of all our pursuits, and snicker at them even as they presented them for our enjoyment.

The conclusion of *Raiders* is a glitch in *The Matrix*. It is a glorious and transcendent moment that communicates that there is far more to the world that is random, and confusing, and infuriating - and beautiful in its inscrutable absurdity - than in all the fantasies of aggression and conquest possible in the noetic brain of the mainstream culture.

And those feelings are the sole defense I can give for the *Deus Ex Machina*.

Perhaps that itching sensation in the back of our collective necks that the problems of a complex and complicated society can't actually be solved by one man and two fists alone is a much needed corrective to the soul-corroding, engagement-killing, anti-intellectual effect of centuries of national myths of rugged individualism.

Perhaps the notion that human failings as difficult as fascism, anti-semitism, militarism, toxic masculinity, and rampant technocratic consumerism will only be solved by God if they are not solved by all of us together is a necessary moral lesson that does not get the air time it deserves - even though Spielberg, Lucas, Kaufman, and Kasdan have provided a dramatically perfect model of how to monetize it for entertainment.

Perhaps the myth of the Great Man as savior of the entire world - though a beguiling and entertaining way to while away an afternoon - is as bad a trap as the evils that overwhelm us in our daily life because it specifically invites the rest of us to sit back, stay out of the fray, and wait for a bullwhip-wielding academic or a group of repentant time-traveling dwarves to show up with armies to save us.

Perhaps showing us that heroes - even when they conquer their own demons - cannot defeat the Ultimate Darkness alone but for the help of God is a way that art can command us all to become that hero for ourselves: and then to find more like us, help them become heroes, and come together to prevent horrors that would otherwise make us pray for the coming of a savior.

Perhaps, after all the gods and heroes have left the stage, all that's left behind is us, alone in truth - but together in ideal - to "carry on the fight."

IS IT JUST ME OR HAVE THE BAD GUYS BEEN KICKING A LOT OF ASS LATELY?

5.31.15

The following contains what people who haven't seen a single mainstream film in the last thirty years may consider spoilers.

If that's you, how did you find this essay, and do our modern ways frighten and confuse you?

U p front I'd like to say that I am pretty much agnostic on *Kingsman: The Secret Service* - even if this rant is in apropos of my viewing of that film. Like many of its genre, I enjoyed some of *Kingsman* and also found much of it politically problematic and - more damningly - smug. I suspect, given *Kingsman's* overall level of "cheek," that most of the problematic aspects were very much intentional - and putatively satirical - provocations.

What struck me most forcefully about *Kingsman* was how much the third act - in which the villain unleashes a plot to turn the entire population of the earth into hyper-aggressive psychotics who violently turn on one other, thus triggering a massive genocidal cleansing of our overpopulated planet - was, in spite of the film's insistence on its cheeky subversion of the accepted tropes of the spy film, completely typical for this kind of filmmaking in the past decade.

Like pretty much every other film in which the stakes are "save the world," *Kingsman* and its "heroes" settle not so much for saving it, as much as "preventing it from getting fucked up ALL the way."

For approximately twenty minutes of the final hour of *Kingsman* - and, again, I am not picking on this film specifically, but merely saying that it is the latest version of this type of storytelling that I have seen - the audience is regaled with some very graphic sequences showing the unfolding of the villain's plan around the world... scenes of hundreds of thousands of civilians murdering one another on the streets of Rio de Janeiro, Los Angeles, and London, with all the attendant collateral damage of car crashes and flaming buildings and crashing airplanes that could be lovingly rendered by the film's CGI budget.

For good measure, *Kingsman* also throws in a set piece in which the heads of most of the governments of the world are explosively decapitated. I assume this was intended as a bit of anti-establishment satire, as the film makes clear that everyone from Barack Obama to the Prime Minister of Sweden are in league with the villain and are merely being hoisted on their own petard for allowing themselves to receive cranial implants from a Blofeldian megalomaniac.

That the hero of the film is rewarded not just with the usual bit of Pussy Galorean slap-and-tickle we have seen forty years of James Bonds receive at the end of their own spy films, but, rather, offered anal sex by one of the crowned heads of Europe as a reward for his service -

which he shows up to take at the end of the film with a bottle of champagne, two flutes and a shit-eating smile - shows not only how far we have come in showing women as transactional objects in mainstream cinema (a tragic and disgusting reality that's tossed off in *Kingsman* as a bit of the aforementioned "cheek") it also sheds a very specific light on how raunch and bro culture has established "anal" as a kind of holy grail for casual sex in spite of the general sexual illiteracy and emotional tone-deafness of the trope... or maybe there was a missing scene where the Kinsgmen's spy gadgets are revealed to have vast hidden reservoirs of lube.

Anyway, I digress. The point I was trying to make is that the raunch/bro-culture fantasy aside, the film's hero is "richly" rewarded for "saving the world" at the end of *Kingsman* when the truth - rendered with hundreds of thousands of dollars of special effects detail - is anything but.

I don't want to get all get-off-my-lawn on you, but as I was watching all this mayhem, I kept wondering what it would be like to go to a convention of villains at some mid-century modern hotel - perhaps in Acapulco, or a Ruritanian ski chalet in Gstaad - and listen to the ones from current films recount their exploits... because, in truth, they wouldn't even have to exercise their ability to spin in order to recast their defeats at the hands of latter-day heroes as massive victories.

Let's face it - given just what was shown onscreen - in *Kingsman*, the villain not only destabilized every government in the world, he probably also caused the deaths of at least a million people - and he's not alone in his success...

In *Man of Steel* - the most recent reimagination of

the Superman Myth - *the* nefarious General Zod easily murdered a quarter million people and destroyed all of metropolis.

In *Captain America: The Winter Soldier*, H.Y.D.R.A. TOTALLY succeed in their plan to cripple S.H.I.E.L.D., destroy their entire infrastructure, and crash two ARC reactor-powered flying aircraft carriers into the Potomac: no doubt killing tens of thousands, but also polluting one of the nation's most iconic waterways for decades to come and - perhaps - rendering the area uninhabitable.

The villain of *Star Trek Into Darkness* - and frankly, I can't remember whether it was Khan, Old Robocop, or James T. Kirk (there's a good argument to be made for any one of them) - certainly pulled off the nigh-impossible task of crashing a city-sized starship with two antimatter-rich warp cores into downtown San Francisco - again, most likely murdering tens if not hundreds of thousands.

In Michael Bay's *Transformers oeuvre,* all sanity, reason, and accountability are smashed into oblivion... and that's just in the theaters showing the movies (tadum-dum!).

In *The Dark Knight Rises*, the League of Shadows not only assassinates countless heads of local government, they also cut off a city the size of New York (combined with Los Angeles, Pittsburgh, and Chicago) from the Federal Government and cause three months of complete anarchy in which the fabric of society is rent asunder and ordinary people resort to horrible acts of gang violence in order to both survive and avenge themselves on the 1%.

Oh, and also - and I can't put too fine a point on it - the villains of *The Dark Knight Rises* fucking KILL BATMAN. (And yes, *Marvel's The Avengers* gets a little free pass for their wholesale destruction of New York City because the filmmakers at least made a concession to the idea that heroes should save the lives of innocents even as they served up heaping dollops of vehicular and architectural carnage - in this respect that film is the best of the lot and I am not above admitting it. So there.)

With that in mind, let's go back to our imaginary super villain summit. Imagine the conversation that might take place between, say, Auric Goldfinger and the Joker from *The Dark Knight*, over a few gimlets at the courtesy bar... "Man has climbed Mount Everest, fired rockets to the Moon, split the atom, achieved miracles in every field of human endeavor - except crime!" "Dang skippy, big guy - and would that I had gotten to see the totality of my evil scheme... but alas all I got to do was blow up a hospital, murder a measly dozen or so people including cops, judges and local politicians, commandeer the local media, cause a city-wide evacuation, take two ferries full of civilians hostage, kidnap the crusading D.A., burn half his body, detonate his fiancee with drums of gasoline, turn him into a spree killer, force the police to open fire on innocent civilians, and crash a helicopter."

At this point, Blofeld drops his drink, prostrates himself before Heath Ledger's Joker, and shouts "I AM NOT WORTHY!"

Later - and perhaps in tears - Goldfinger sheepishly confesses that all he did was fail to irradiate all the gold in Fort Knox.

Of course, such a summit could never happen, because in the great tradition of all these films, the bad guys do tend to get killed off at the end... unless they are being played by Tom Hiddleston and have a multi-film deal.

I also imagine a hero summit held in some dank sub basement where Sean Connery's James Bond - nah, fuck it, not Sean Connery's James Bond, just plain old Sean

Connery: white-haired, wrinkled, and cranky - kicks
the ever-loving shit out of Henry Cavill's Superman
and Christian Bale's Batman with nothing but his bare
knuckles, "Scotland forever" tattoo, and the musk of being
a Real Man, for being such a miserable couple of deadbeats
at saving the lives of innocents.

You get the point.

Up until very recently, the job of the hero was to - in
the words of *Pacific Rim*'s Marshall Stocker Pentecost -
"cancel the apocalypse"...

Nowadays, the job of the hero seems to be to fail to
stop the apocalypse... to let it happen just long enough that
the audience is entertained by the marriage of Irwin Allen
disaster porn and spy / superhero action, and then kill the
bad guy just in time for the innocent civilians to emerge
bruised and battered from the crossfire and - sometime in
the interim between sequels - figure out how to rebuild
the cities, overcome the scorching PTSD that is about to
plummet them into an apocalyptic downward spiral of
depression, social alienation, sleepless nights, and ruined
relationships with their friends and family, clean up the
pollution, keep the atomic power plants from melting
down, and elect new world leaders with some level of
competence in running the political and systems that keep
the society afloat.

And if you think I am overthinking it, here comes the
dry, witless, and unglamorously wide end of my wedge:
my belief that this trend in our popular culture is yet
another damning indicator of our nation's immoral and
juvenile response to the terror attacks of 9-11.

There is a line in the film *The Matrix Reloaded* which,
somewhat surprisingly, stuck with me; it's in the scene
where Neo meets the Architect of the Matrix, who explains

that even if Neo chooses to destroy the Matrix - which we have been told would be victory for his side - "there are levels of survival we are willing to accept."

In a way, the destruction we all witnessed live on TV in 9-11 turned our entertainment from mere heroic fantasy to "resigned disaster porn/heroic fantasy."

A truth came into our lives in an undeniable and horrific way on September 11th: we are members of the global community as both victims and aggressors. On that day, we became no different from any other country with a long and varied history of good and bad foreign policy dealing with horrific blowback from the latter.

Rather than process the horror and respond with a mature level of introspection - and a commensurate amount of investigation and prosecution of the guilty - our leaders simply encouraged us to continue living our lives (lest "the terrorists win"), return to our shopping malls and resorts as soon as possible (lest our economy falter), and let a few government-canonized heroes (and a lot of faceless expendables) pursue a fantasy of harsh vengeance on shores much further than our own...

And of course, that in our fear and anxiety, we were willing to give up many basic freedoms in exchange for the blood of faceless heroes and villains, and write our government a blank check to "build democracy" by doling obscenely large defense and homeland security contracts to their cronies (and this is where the anal sex metaphor comes in VERY handy), so much the better.

That our popular culture responded to this mandate by simultaneously doubling-down on the depiction of wholesale destruction while perpetuating our collective desire for revenge - and giving up on the notion that heroes should be heroes and not just grim-faced machines of reprisal - should surprise no one.

On the day that Real Life let us know with both feet that - our technological superiority and perceived moral authority notwithstanding - even the mighty U.S. of A. can't stop a sufficiently clever and motivated adversary from taking a bloody piece of us, we collectively settled for entertainment that does exactly what we did in real life: pursue the murder of the villain by the hand of the audience-surrogate hero without caring how many deaths take place in the process, or how the world fixes itself (just that it happens in time for the sequel). "The audience now knows from real life that even heroes can't stop the countdown clock before the bomb explodes," our modern action/adventure/thriller/superhero films tell us, "but what if we sell the audience on the notion that it doesn't matter? Why don't we just make the hero so exceptional that his own survival - even in the face of the senseless deaths of thousands - is enough to justify the perception of him as the hero?"

To me, the protagonists of these films are a sad, sorry stand-in for a morally vertiginous America and its allies: indifferent to the suffering of victims, numb to collateral damage, and insensitive to the destruction of what in the real world would be the accomplishments of millions... and it's all because A. It looks so darned pretty on the screen where the endless pyrokinetics of stunts and visual effects keep the destruction abstract and none of it touches our perception of reality in any meaningful way, B. No one identifies with the pixillated mobs of CGI citizens and everyone (even women and minorities, believe it or not) wants to identify with the Great White Avenger... and, most importantly, C. The villains in films are always clearly the villains - no need to delve into the complexities of foreign policy cause-and-effect in mainstream, mass-audience wish-fulfillment.

In short, sons-a-bitches had it coming, and that's that.

The delusion is simple and seductive: as long as I'm a hero in pursuit of a villain, nothing else matters. Quoth the machine overlords: "There are levels of survival we are willing to accept."

Or maybe it's just that we live in a world where the prevalence of villainy hides in plain sight by numbing us to its presence with a slow upward climb in temperature - and by "temperature" I mean willful blindness to our own brutality, complacence, and general malfeasance in the pursuit of political power at any cost - heretofore reserved for frogs in pots of boiling water.

How strange, then, that as this trend in popular entertainment matures to become *status quo*, that the films bucking the trend are, in fact, the James Bond movies. *Casino Royale* ended with a poker game and a fight in a crumbling building… *Quantum of Solace* climaxed with fisticuffs between Daniel Craig and the scrawny, Roman Polanski-looking dude from Th*e Diving Bell and the Butterfly* in a hotel lobby… and *Skyfall* contented itself with a climactic - and slightly less sadistic - remaking of the last act of *Home Alone*.

Hell, compared to the large scale carnage seen in *Man of Steel*, *Skyfall* feels like one of the quieter, more meditative, Ingmar Bergman movies.

And let's face it - it makes sense that James Bond should still be stopping the bad guys from messing up the world too badly… because if he doesn't, what is he?

The melancholy last son of Krypton who can never return home?

The tragic heir to a vast fortune with unlimited

personal resources with which to fight crime?

The teenager whose alienation has only been increased by the acquisition of superpowers and who must now also learn the meaning of duty and sacrifice?

The finder of an alien artifact that allows him to control an army of mechanical beasts disguised as cars?

No. If James Bond fails, he's just a violent, middle-aged, alcoholic sociopath.

And that's the strange part of it: the hero who bears the standard of one of the most classist and imperialist societies of the past five hundred years is the only one who actually has to sing for his supper, being as he has no idealized backstory entitlement on which to lean.

Compared to Superman, Batman, Captain America, Iron Man, Thor, and all the other American-made superheroes, England's James Bond is a public servant who actually has to answer to someone on pain of being fired from his job. If he lets that Earth-ending countdown clock run down to zero, he has to go on the dole!

As the product of a country already acclimated to terrorist bombing campaigns on the home soil, many decades of humbling decolonization - and the systematic breaking down of a once-thought-infinite system of class, entitlement, and peerage - the latter-day Bond films have found themselves needing to establish some sort of personal investment in the hero to invalidate the need for such widespread mayhem.

At least for now, the days of James Bond fighting mad (and usually vulgar and self-made) bourgeois industrialists hellbent on destroying the world via misattributed nuclear missile strikes, satellites able to turn entire cities into molten wastelands, and the mass extinction of humanity through poisoning via orchid extract delivered from an orbiting space station in the name of his noble overlords, have gone the way of his homeland's collective denial, anger, bargaining, depression, and acceptance about the end of Empire.

From that example, then, I put forth the suggestion that maybe we American screenwriters should be just a little, teeny-weeny bit more humble in crafting our own overblown spectacles of vicarious revenge, and apply our creativity to the development of character and not spectacle... or at least to seeing if there's a way to go back to that countdown clock that stops at 00:000:07 before the atomic bomb actually explodes and fucks our shit up.

I mean, come on. We're all creative people here. There must to be more ways of skinning that cat. There has to be some way to keep the old tropes of action, adventure, excitement - and, yes, even bloody satisfaction - alive while sparing the audience from endless re-traumatizing recreations of the collapsing buildings, falling innocents, and billowing clouds of fire that we all saw on 9-11.

But if that's too lofty a goal, then let me just offer this one morsel as food for thought to anyone contemplating that state of modern American action/adventure: if James Bond is your last remaining symbol of sanity, then, in the immortal words of Harry Dean Stanton in *Marvel's The Avengers*..."Son, you've got a condition."

I HAVE NO OPINION ABOUT *STAR WARS, EPISODE VIII: THE LAST JEDI*

(a.k.a. "OBLIGATORY STAR WARS THINK PIECE, 2017 EDITION)
Originally Published at ForcesOfGeek.com, 2.22.17

I have a dirty and shameful secret to share with you: I have no opinion about *Star Wars, Episode VIII: The Last Jedi*.

Now - when I first saw *Star Wars, Episode VIII: The Last Jedi* (which, for the record, was less than a week ago) I had a metric shit-ton of opinions, which I gleefully shared in the form of lengthy arguments with my friends on social media. For many in my generation, having opinions about *Star Wars* is kind of like having oxygen, and the more extreme and passionately argued those opinions the better.

Then I went to see *Star Wars, Episode VIII: The Last Jedi* a second time. It has been my tradition to see these movies at least twice in a theater since I was seven years old. Having sated my thirst to have a strongly stated opinion about *Star Wars, Episode VIII: The Last Jedi* in the week following its release, I found myself walking out of the theater from my second viewing with no opinion at all.

Is it a good movie? A bad movie?

I honestly don't know.

And it is in the not knowing that I have found how I truly feel about this film - and all the many *Star Wars*es that have come before and will undoubtedly come after.--

One of the hardest moments I have had in a writers room came a few years back on a deeply serialized series which I had struggled to master. After pitching an episodic story I had spent the better part of a week developing with the rest of the staff to one of my colleagues - hoping for a blessing to take the story up the flagpole to the showrunner - my colleague shook his head and, with much sympathy told me "It's not that it's not a story, it's that I only see The Churn."

If you can imagine me walking out of that room with my head downcast and the "sad Charlie Brown" music from the old animated specials playing, you have an idea of the aftermath...

And as I walked out of my second viewing of *Star Wars, Episode VIII: The Last Jedi*, my colleague's turn of phrase hung over my head like a hangman's noose.

The Churn.--

The Churn - I've come to believe - is what happens to all "tentpole" movie franchises. The Churn is what happens to all television shows that overstay their operational life before exhausting their fanbase's appetite for the characters. The Churn is what must happen for comic books, soap operas - and the works of countless fantasy novelists - to exist.

The Churn is the river into which those who want to make a fortune from narrative storytelling must wade... and the rapids which they must survive.

The Churn, is - for both good and bad - the constant invention, reinvention, escalation, re-escalation, doubling down, and re-doubling down of concept and incident that must take place in order for long-term narratives to endure. The Churn is what you get when the property makes money and there is no end in sight.

The Churn is the latest chase, abduction, or standoff; the new villain, and the new love interest. The Churn is the reboot, the preboot, the prequel, the sequel and the equal.

The Churn is what audiences get when stories go from being "a story with a beginning, a middle, and an end" to being like life: an endless series of obstacles, setbacks, repetitions of behaviors good and bad, relapses into behaviors both good and bad, deaths, births, and comings and goings, with little hope of a real resolution. The Churn is when the myth of Odysseus - something with a defined beginning, middle, and end - morphs into the myth of Sisyphus - an endless challenge that can never be completed.--

With *Star Wars*, The Churn has been with us a long time, even if the mainstream audience does not realize it. The Churn kept *Star Wars* alive in the dark days between *Star Wars, Episode IV: Return of the Jedi* and *Star Wars, Episode I: The Phantom Menace*.

During these years, over 400 *Star Wars* novels, e-books, and comic books were released. In absence of filmed *Star Wars* product, the faithful filled their story-craving bellies with a stream of titles beginning with Timothy Zahn's (justly) venerated "Thrawn Trilogy" and culminating with the 19-novel epic serial *Star Wars: The New Jedi Order*.

In the course of these narratives, the character known as Luke Skywalker was married (to a subaltern of his arch-nemesis Emperor Palpatine, no less), imprisoned (in almost every story - usually with a fiendishly clever trap that somehow nullified his Jedi abilities), promoted, demoted, turned into a gladiator, tempted to join the Dark Side, eventually made to join the Dark Side and apprenticed to a clone of Emperor Palpatine, forced into a lightsaber battle against his own clone (the somewhat comically named "Luuke"), made deathly ill multiple times, cut off from the force multiple times, sired a child, forced to reckon with his faulty knowledge of the totality of the force (also several times), built and destroyed several Jedi temples, had his wife become deathly ill several times, forced into exile, forced to ally with his deadly foes - The Sith - to defeat a common enemy, almost had to abandon his son when his mind was overtaken by the telepathic ability of a colony of insectoid aliens, and blown up imperial planet-killing weapons by the metric ton. It would be fair to say that Luke Skywalker has been subject to more dramatic incident in the form of life-or-death situations than any human being could possibly face while remaining sane.

And that was all before Disney purchased Lucasfilm and all of its assets and declared the entire kit and kaboodle null and void. All the old publications (known as the "Expanded Universe") were rebranded as "Star Wars Legends" and a whole new set of novels detailing an entire alternate life for our hero has been in motion for years now. Of course, the "Star Wars Legends" have remained in print for anyone who wants to read newly non-canonical *Star Wars* fiction. There's still gold in them thar hills.

I bring all of this up to illustrate two points.

One, where there is money to be made with characters for which an audience has a bottomless craving, the gods of commerce will have no problem commissioning hundreds of artists to create as many adventures for those characters as humanly possible: and those adventures will all have a slew of tropes in common, eventually becoming a repetitive cycle of Philip Glassian proportions.

There will always be another rogue Jedi who has been in hiding, another bounty hunter with strange powers that boggle those who rely on The Force, another brilliant officer of the Galactic Empire with a plan so dangerous (usually involving a heretofore unknown planet-killing weapon hidden by Emperor Palpatine before his death) that it could mean the fate of the galaxy (in at least one occasion, it was a double of a brilliant officer who was propped up by other brilliant officers in order to use his PR value as a brilliant officer to revive the Galactic Empire).

In short... The Churn.

My second point is that, as I went whole hog into the game of having opinions about *Star Wars, Episode VIII: The Last Jedi*, I kept hearing otherwise sane people railing vitriolic about how awful it was "what they did to Luke Skywalker!" Which is kinda hilarious, considering all that has already been done to Luke Skywalker in the name of "keeping the franchise alive."

In the name of The Churn.

It has been at least three decades since *Star Wars* entered The Churn - and it has never looked back. The relative quality of each new installment, regardless of media or venue, is pretty much insignificant at this point because everyone who loves *Star Wars* (which nowadays seems to be not just the entire civilized world, but also all the jocks who used to beat me up for liking *Star Wars*) has a constant lifeline to *Star Wars* that will continue to churn new material as quickly as possible.

And in the thick of The Churn, there's another churn: The Churn of public narratives about the behind the scenes of *Star Wars*... and make no mistake, the stories of the making of *Star Wars* - and what it "means" that *Star Wars* is being made, and by whom - is as important to keeping the franchise alive as the movies themselves.

That Churn demands that we occasionally be sold

the idea that the latest piece of Star Wars product is "a revitalization" of the source material: as is the case with the latest and greatest. Much of the press around *Star Wars, Episode VII: The Last Jedi* centers around the promotional narrative that this is a "bold reimagination" of a franchise; that a new *auteur* writer/director has been given the reins and infused the entire enterprise with new life, new ideas, and such newfound wisdom that this will not only register to the faithful as a pleasant return to a beloved universe, but also blow the collective mind with its sheer newness.

Meaning no disrespect - and making no judgment about the quality of *Star Wars, Episode VIII: The Last Jedi* - I just don't buy it.

Why? Because of The Churn.

For forty years of my life *Star Wars* has been a self-contained ecosystem with its own predatory megafauna. Both within the story and without, those of us who care enough to stand under the bombs have been continually shelled with promises that each forthcoming novel/book/comic/e-book/TV movie/animated series/animated series pilot turned theatrical release/series of animated shorts/movie is a "bold reimagination" of our beloved space opera; that each new creator has brought to it Something Remarkable, and we will be blown away.

Of course that's never really the case.

Here's what invariably happens in all Star Wars stories, "bold reimagination" or not...

The Jedi knights/rebellion/New Republic/New Jedi Order get in a bind created by a former Imperial officer trying to restore Palpatine's glory/a rogue Jedi who escaped the purges and went into hiding only to be twisted by the Dark Side/the First Order/The Yuuzhan Vong/a clone of Palpatine/a Grand Moff who sat out the Galactic

Civil War. The galaxy is threatened. Someone is abducted. There's a light saber duel/starship battle. There's a few twists and turns in which some character you could have sworn was evil or good makes a dramatic reversal. The balance of the Force comes into question (perhaps with some "daring" and "new" ideas about how The Force works and that there really is no Dark or Light side)...

And the status quo is eventually restored after, perhaps, some significant loss - but not of a member of the core ensemble. (Up until it became necessary for Disney to kill the increasingly crotchety, septuagenarian Han Solo in order to convince the increasingly crotchety, septuagenarian Harrison Ford to return for one last go in the racing stripe trousers, the only time *Star Wars* even remotely made good on killing one of our beloved heroes was in "Vector Prime" the first novel of the "New Jedi Order" series... in which they dropped an entire FUCKING MOON on poor Chewbacca to prove that the bad guys meant business.)

(No really. They meant it. Business.)

(And if you think what they did to Admiral Ackbar in *Star Wars, Episode VIII: The Last Jedi* was an outrage, to me it seemed far less ignominious than his arrest and imprisonment for embezzlement (?!?) at the beginning of *Heir to the Empire*.)

So the business of *Star Wars* churns on... having done so for four decades without any real signs of stopping.

Entire literary canons consisting of hundreds of works have been excised from the mainstream narrative and replaced with new histories, films have been remastered, re-edited, and re-visual-effected, entire technologies have been invented to allow us to experience the original - and new works - in ways we never could before, new canons are being invented, and the characters from the originals - and the increasingly superannuated actors who play them - are being gracefully allowed to bow out in favor of exciting new characters...

Who happen to be a young, force-sensitive person whose raw power means a rebirth of the Jedi Order, a rogue pilot whose ability with the stick far outpaces his judgment and wisdom, a couple of droids, a couple of cute aliens, a masked and mysterious character who doesn't amount to much, a dark lord who is conflicted about his commitment to evil, and a loyal friend who will remain true through thick and thin.

You may, at this point, be thinking that my rehashing the old chestnut that "there is nothing new under the sun" is a gateway to a declaration that I am somehow above enjoying *Star Wars* and that I have achieved a higher plane of consciousness and need to let you know it.

Let me reassure you. Having read the majority of the 400 publications mentioned earlier, and having seen *Star Wars, Episode VIII: The Last Jedi* on opening night, and knowing that I will see it multiple more times - nothing could be further from the truth. Look, *Star Wars* is so crucial to my being that one time, <u>I had to go cold turkey from it for a year to prove to myself that there was more to me than *Star Wars*</u>.

While I have made my peace with *Star Wars* and still enjoy it, I could not do so without acknowledging that the pleasure centers of my brain that received it so eagerly for decades are no longer firing as brightly as they once did.

Also, it would be disingenuous to dismiss a franchise because of The Churn... because, as with all things having to do with the magic of creation, The Churn is neither all bad nor all good. Not everyone has had *Star Wars* in their life as long as others. One person's feeling that they are merely in The Churn of a story that has to be kept on life support in the name of profit is another person's first step into a much larger world.

Let's face it: there are people out there for whom Kathryn Janeway was their first *Star Trek* captain - and the best in their mind. There are those who swear that Pierce Brosnan is the greatest Bond ever. There are those for whom Chris Pine's Captain Kirk is THE Kirk (and that Shatner guy is just some old weirdo who trolls people on Twitter).

There are even people out there for whom Colin Baker is the ONE TRUE DOCTOR.

As the sales pitch on *Star Wars, Episode VIII: The Last Jedi* gives way to countless reports of its success in comparison to other *Star Wars* product - and to countless analyses of how it was received by the public - the public narrative has come to echo one the film's core thematic concerns. Apparently, a lot of O.G. *Star Wars* fans who are excessively attached to the old ways are unhappy with the movie's bold and reinventing ways, and have been vocal about it.

Concomitantly, newer fans wish that we O.G. *Star Wars* geezers would stop having opinions about our beloved characters and stop grousing about the boldness of reinvention on display. The film, after all, is about how the old must give way to the new, and the geezers who once sought to save the galaxy must acknowledge the truth that the galaxy still needs saving, and the people to do this must be given lease to build on the old legacy.

I, for one, am willing to do that.

Seriously. I have no beef with anything that has been done to the old characters, or how the uniforms and costumes have been changed, or the spaceships redesigned, or any such thing. The Churn needs fodder, just like the spice must flow.

But what I do ask you give this old geezer in trade is an acknowledgement: that you can understand how it might be a little hard for me to believe that *Star Wars* will ever be bold, new, reimagined, or turbocharged by a new creative auteur/team of auteurs with ideas so radical that they will make me see the universe in a new way.

Star Wars has always been rife with new beginnings, new directions, and new ideas... but it really has never been all that good with endings. The laws of business pretty much dictate that *Star Wars* must never have a conclusive ending.

As long as we pay good money for those tickets, and the novels, and the comic books, and the spinoff animated series, and the streaming service that carries the spinoff animated series, The Churn will churn will churn will churn.

You're probably thinking that I'm being melodramatic. I mean, hey, the end of *Star Wars: Episode VI - Return of the Jedi* felt pretty conclusive and emotionally gratifying. And it was. Hell, it even featured a curtain call...

Until a few years later, when Uncle George stuck us with the prequels. And then a few years after that, when Disney bought the franchise and the First Order arose from the Dark Side with a great deal of the Empire's livery and haberdashery intact.

That livery and haberdashery - Jedi robes, Stormtrooper armor, Darth Vader's samurai-inspired helmet - are part of a set of icons so powerful that it has sustained the touch of many, many artists - simultaneously delivering a message of hope while constantly mustering

challenge after challenge to that hope, all in the name
of The Churn. Whatever else anyone has to say about
Star Wars, I don't know a single artist who doesn't
wish - usually with a great and envious fury - to invent
something as simple yet universally evocative - and
provocative of heroic dreams - as a light saber.

We go to *Star Wars* because its symbols trigger
powerful, primal, and archetypal emotions that often
transcend the need for such things as good dialogue,
cohesive plotting, and characters who are consistent in
their *raisons d'être*.

It all comes down to this: *Star Wars, Episode VIII: The
Last Jedi* may boldly - but mostly loudly - declaim its intent
to "let the past die"... but the past ain't going anywhere.

In this case, the legend of Odysseus has been the myth
of Sisyphus for a very long time, and what so many of
us now realize is that the Dark Side will never fall. The
Empire - and all of its ilk - will never be conclusively
defeated. There will always be a planet-killing super
weapon lurking behind some heretofore uncharted nebula.

Star Wars is no longer heroic aspirational fiction. *Star
Wars* is now pretty much exactly like life. A thing that just
keeps happening to people.

And because The Churn is an endless river, some will
step into it for the first time and absolutely feel that they
are seeing something bold and new. I envy them, as I envy
those for whom that endless river is an infinite source of
satisfaction.

There's nothing wrong with continuing to love
something that just keeps going. Icons are important,
symbols are important, the idea of hope is important. The
great thing about *Star Wars* is that most viewers will be
done with it long before it is done with them - and for

those who choose to leave, it will just keep going in their absence, lying in wait for the moment when the heart grows fonder.

For some of us who live *Star Wars* - and have loved it since the beginning - the consumption of these narratives is much like going to a once surprising, and now frequently remodeled, restaurant where we can always get a table and have tasted everything on the menu. It would take a very serious screwing of the pooch on behalf of the constantly-changing management for the meal to be truly awful, and on those occasions when the food isn't up to par, the discussion of the whys and hows of that failure with our fellow regulars are every bit as entertaining as the product itself.

So I have no opinion about *Star Wars, Episode VIII: The Last Jedi*.

Is it good? Sure. Is it bad? Sure. Is it *Star Wars*? Sure. It says so on the package, and a lot of far less deserving material has carried the same label and been accepted as such, so why not this one too?

Was there ever any doubt that I was going to show up on opening night and be ready to engage my fellow geeks in heated discussion of its particulars?

Absolutely not.

And so it will be for the foreseeable future... or at least until the day comes when some young artist pulls off a feat worthy of the son of a stationery store owner from Modesto, California and creates (with the help of great collaborators, nascent technology, and a popular culture ready for a sea change in the types of subject matter it considers worthy of mass appeal) a story so chock full of transcendent iconography that it eclipses everything else in the media imagination with the bright and shining appearance of that most hallowed of commodities - newness.

Then perhaps *Star Wars* will do that thing it keeps promising to do. That thing it cannot do while fortunes are being made and people are willing to accept the sales pitch that every subsequent iteration is something previously unseen.

That thing that will truly - and conclusively - earn it a place in the ranks of the greatest stories ever told...

It will end.

I REJECT YOUR REALITY AND SUBSTITUTE MY OWN

5.31.16

*B*lade Runner may be a seminal text of filmed science fiction, but its visual genius is only matched by the conceptual muddle that director Ridley Scott has spent years making of its central dramatic question.

Philip K. Dick's novel *Do Androids Dream of Electric Sheep* is reasonably clear about what it is about: a depressed man whose wife hates him for not making enough money in his job as a bounty hunter to buy the family a status symbol (which, in Dick's bombed-out post-nuclear dystopia, is a real animal to keep as a pet; the family must make do with fooling the neighbors with a lifelike robotic sheep) is forced to murder runaway androids masquerading as people to make more money to buy a real sheep, only to learn from the androids' relentless efforts to survive his hunt that they are not all that much different than he is... all they want is to live and experience happiness, or a reasonable simulacrum thereof.

Ultimately, the answer to the titular question is that you're missing the point. What matters is that they dream.

In turning Dick's novel into a film (if Paul Sammon's making-of book *Future Noir* is to be believed), David Peoples wrote a line in a late-stage draft of the script in which Deckard - having taken down Roy Batty, the last of his bounty - ponders the soul-destroying nature of his state-sanctioned serial murder, and muses that while his synthetic prey (now called "replicants" instead of "androids") all know their maker, he has no idea who or what made him:

> *"I wonder who designs the ones like me .*
> *. . the great Tyrell hadn't designed me, but*
> *whoever had hadn't done so much better. In*
> *my own modest way, I was a combat model.*
> *Roy Batty was my late brother..."* [3]

Finding the poetics of that line of dialogue utterly beguiling, Ridley Scott proceeded to conceive the idea that it would be a cool mindfuck if Rick Deckard was also a replicant. And thus, thirty years of directorial retconning of the established theme of Philip K. Dick's work was born.

Because he came to this epiphany late in the process, Ridley Scott has spent the decades since the release of the original theatrical version of *Blade Runner* tinkering with his movie to bolster the idea of Deckard-as-replicant. Changing a visual here, a special effects shot there, adding a subtle hint that Deckard may be a replicant here, taking away evidence that he might be human there, Scott has slowly, and over the years, done his level best to retroactively rewrite his work into something different than was originally intended. As a result, there are now a large number of commercially-released versions of the film, all the way down to an official "final" cut (don't you believe it) which was put out to coincide with the film's thirtieth anniversary.

---

3   Sammon, Paul, *Future Noir: The Making of Blade Runner* (New York, Harper Collins/Dey St., 2017), Chapter XVII - The Director's Cut, subsection: (Kindle Edition, page number unavailable).

The verdict from the "final" cut is that Rick Deckard is - at least in the Ridley Scott film version of *Do Androids Dream of Electric Sheep?* - in fact, a replicant.

But here's the thing, when you buy the "final" cut, you also have the option of acquiring a bundle with up to five other versions of the movie - beginning with a workprint with temp music and incomplete VFX work - in which Deckard is either more or less of a replicant depending on where in his belief that Deckard was a replicant Ridley Scott was at the time he made each different version of the film.

The "final" result of all this tinkering is that our poor, put-upon Rick Deckard - who still has to do the shit work of killing sentient beings for a living after losing a wife and an electric sheep in the translation from novel to cinema - is the sad victim of what can only be understood as a thoroughly "Phildickian" identity crisis. A capricious god has brought into existence numerous versions of Rick Deckard, all of them slightly different, and all of them at variable levels of proximity to the undeniable - if nonsensical-within-the-narrative-frame-of-the-film-and-source-material - possibility that he may not, be a human being. Or may. Depending on which version you watch.

It also bears mentioning here that the words "Blade Runner" do not, in fact, appear in Philip K. Dick's novel - Scott thought that Deckard's job description as "bounty hunter" or "detective" was far too prosaic and asked Hampton Fancher to come up with something sexier. When Fancher stumbled upon a copy of a William Burroughs movie treatment entitled *Blade Runner* - which apparently was a futuristic story of medical supplies smugglers - Scott found the word combination cool and directed the production company to pay Burroughs for the rights to the title. I only bring this up, because when you add to the possibility that our suppositious Rick Deckard not only faces an extraordinary crisis of identity, but is also trapped in a reality which had been thoroughly misnamed in an effort to make it appear more exciting than it was ever intended, the truly viscous nature of his existence comes all that more into focus.

Now those of us in the "geek community" have been having some - usually drunken - version of the "does it make sense if Rick Deckard is a replicant" argument pretty much ever week for the past thirty years.

My side of it goes a little something like this:

If Rachael, the replicant Deckard falls in love with in the film, is - as Doctor Tyrell, the head of the corporation that manufactures the replicants explains - a unique experiment for having been implanted with the memories of Tyrell's own niece in order to give her a false sense of her own humanity, then why and when would/could the Tyrell corporation go so far as to create another unique replicant with a lifetime of unique memories and place him in the police force unit responsible for hunting replicants? How is Rachael an "experiment" if Tyrell already has at least one, if not more, fully functional replicants on the police beat each with their own bizarre memories of unicorns (a running theme in the dream and memory sequences in the films)?

The usual reply goes a little something like this:

Duh. Because killing for a job is too psychologically taxing and dehumanizing a line of work for anyone, so the Tyrell corporation partnered secretly with the police to put replicants in the job in order to keep ordinary people from having to face that horror.

Okay, now here's me calling bullshit... ready?

That's bullshit.

Also, the entire theme of the source material is that killing for a job is a dehumanizing pursuit... why add to Dick's already classic expression of that truth the added layer of convolution that Rick Deckard is a replicant?

Truth: *Auteur* director Ridley Scott made a rash decision based on a single line of (ultimately unused) dialogue that put him at odds with the theme of the film he was making.

And let's be real, anyone who has seen *Prometheus* knows just how much Ridley Scott cares for the internal consistency of canon in narrative.

Now there's been an announcement that Ridley Scott will be producing a sequel to *Blade Runner,* to be directed by Denis Villeneuve, and starring Ryan Gosling... and that Harrison Ford has been confirmed to have a major role in this new production.

OK - wait a minute - how does that even work?

Harrison Ford is over seventy years old, but in *Blade Runner*, it's established that replicants have a four-year lifespan. Now, people who believe that Deckard is a replicant might answer that only SOME replicants have a four-year lifespan, and that part of Rachael's experimental programming is that she had an unlimited lifespan. So it's totally possible that replicant Deckard might also have an unlimited lifespan - right?

Wrong: The other side argues that makes no sense because that's only true of SOME versions of the movie, and that the versions of the movie in which Rachael has an unlimited lifespan are also the ones in which Deckard is LESS likely to be a replicant, since the "unlimited lifespan" concept was expounded only in a much derided voice-over that the studio forced Ridley Scott to put in the original theatrical release of the film... and which he removed in his "director's cut" (not to be confused with his "final" cut) some fifteen years after the original release.

Also, again, if Rachael is so unique as a replicant that all the unicorn imagery in the film represents either her unique gift of memory implants cribbed from Tyrell's niece, or her unique gift of an unlimited lifespan, then if Deckard is a replicant - and also has an unlimited lifespan and also has memories - why the fuck is the central symbol of the film a unicorn? Maybe it should have been a "bi-corn"... or a "multi-corn" depending on how many Rick Deckard replicants are running around.

Or maybe *auteur* director Ridley Scott made a rash decision based on a single line of (ultimately unused) dialogue that put him at odds with the theme of the film he was making.

Once again, I give you Exhibit A. *Prometheus*...

See, on some levels of soft canonicity (if you believe that transmedia advertising campaigns are in fact part of the mythology of the narrative film they advertise) *Prometheus* takes place in the SAME universe as *Blade Runner* - even though the androids in both *Alien*, *Aliens*, *Alien³*, and *Alien Resurrection* (the latter two of which are about to be struck out of the *Alien* canon, or at least shunted aside, in Neill Blomkamp's also recently announced, Ridley Scott-produced soft-non-reboot-sequel of the franchise) are not that hard to tell from people - unlike their *Blade Runner* brethren - because they bleed milk and their innards resemble a cum-stained sack of bits of the old "Capsela" construction toy.

Of course, none of this invalidates the possibility that Harrison Ford may appear in a *Blade Runner* sequel (does that also make it an *Alien* prequel, or an *Alien vs. Predator* sequel?) as:

A.   A later replicant manufactured with Deckard's memories and an unlimited lifespan... or...

B.   The actual dude that Rick Deckard was based on, much as Charles Bishop Weyland was the template for the "Bishop" android/synthetics in the *Alien* franchise...

Of course, that possibility only holds if you believe that *Alien vs. Predator* is canon in the *Blade Runner* universe, or if you believe that the character played by Lance Henriksen in *Alien³* was in fact the real person on whom the Bishop androids - played by Lance Henriksen in *Aliens* - were based... not that that could be possible, since Lance Henriksen played the character on whom the Bishop androids were based in *Alien vs. Predator*, which was set several centuries before *Alien³*.

There are two major conclusions to be drawn from these exertions. First, it is an undeniable truth that Ridley Scott is a fucking menace - at least where canonical integrity is concerned - and that he makes Leiji Matsumoto look like J.K. Rowling.

The other inevitable conclusion is that for the last thirty years, the narrative that a film director named "Ridley Scott" ever made an adaptation of Philip K. Dick's novel *Do Androids Dream of Electric Sheep* has been a false flag operation to cover up a much greater cultural experiment.

In this inevitable conclusion, poor Rick Deckard, which his hectoring wife - or the lack thereof - with his electric sheep - or the lack thereof - with his humanity - or the lack thereof - was never Rick Deckard...

He is, in fact, Joe Chip... an ordinary schmoe trapped in a vast, active, living, intelligent, systems-wide, transmedia-adaptation of the Philip K. Dick novel *UBIK*...

And if Rick Deckard is, in fact, not merely a Philip K. Dick character by dint of being the protagonist of a Philip K. Dick novel, and its continually shape-shifting, mistitled cinematic adaptation, but also the protagonist of a polyvariant narrative adapted from another Philip K. Dick novel... one in which his many incarnations are in a broader conflict to figure out which one inhabits the truest of all their realities... then Ridley Scott can only be Glenn Runciter - Joe Chip's boss in *UBIK*, who may, or may not, have ever been in control of his own reality matrix, and may in fact be dead, unless he is alive, in which case he still may not be Glenn Runciter, but may in fact be God, or a false god set up by our own memories of God, who may or may not exist at all...

In that case, one might add what is *Blade Runner*? Was *Blade Runner* ever truly *Blade Runner* - or even *Do Androids Dream of Electric Sheep*? As the layers come loose, one might consider that *Blade Runner* may not even be a movie... or a consumer product of any kind...

Perhaps *Blade Runner* is *UBIK*... and *UBIK* may be a consumer product, like a floor wax, or a desert topping... or *UBIK* may be Glen Runciter posing as a god...

Or *UBIK* may be God...

Or *UBIK* may be both those things, or all of them simultaneously...

In which case, this is merely the beginning.

SYMPATHY FOR THE MOTION SICKNESS

Originally Published in The Book Smugglers Almanac,
September 2016
8.21.16, Revised 11.8.17

W hen I was young, and far more willing to throw things I didn't fully understand under the bus to score points in arguments about the merits of sci-fi franchises, I would call *Star Trek: The Motion Picture* "Star Trek: The Motion Sickness".

I know - HILARIOUS - right?

However, as I continue to careen down the wormhole of not-so dignified middle age, I have come to appreciate *Star Trek: The Motion Picture* more and more. Though the reason for my appreciation can certainly be blamed in part for its connection to my childhood, and its place in a pop culture body of work I have loved for decades, a lot of it has to do with a growing awareness of everything that *Star Trek: The Motion Picture* is not.

The case against *The Motion Picture* (heretofore shortened to *TMP*) has been made repeatedly. Detractors call it a ponderous, nigh-plotless dirge in which characters who were perfectly entertaining on television were bled of all their vitality and humor in an attempt to project gravitas.

Even at the time of its release, the film's title post-script "The Motion Picture" felt like a pretentious sigil of these flaws: especially since, only a year earlier, Superman, that most iconic of American pop-cultural symbols, settled for the significantly cuddlier (and more promising-of-fun) titular post-script "The Movie."

After watching *TMP* several times in the 80s and 90s, I eventually resolved to consign it to memory during a time when I was busily distancing myself from many of the things I loved in childhood. I even wrote an essay called "<u>My Year Without Star Wars</u>" to explain why this was necessary. However - as time wore on - I figured that an evening spent revisiting the risible and bloated spectacle whose only redeeming value for me had become that it only failed badly enough to beget *Star Trek II: The Wrath of Khan* would be something approximating a good time.

I would be remiss if I didn't mention at this point that, in preparation for this, I devoured a medical-grade marijuana brownie the size of which can only be described as monolithic.

As a syrupy cannabinoid fog descended upon my brain, I fired up my DVD of the "Special Director's Edition" of *TMP* and pressed play. In a minute, my living room filled with the high romance of Jerry Goldsmith's overture.

That's right. As if the film's title didn't already promise a lengthy spell of portentous tedium, *TMP* would also be the last film for almost two decades (until Quentin Tarantino revived the tradition for his film *The Hateful Eight*) released with an <u>overture:</u> signifying for all within earshot that this was not merely a spinoff of a television show widely mocked for low production values and an over-emoting lead actor, but rather a Cultural Event on par with the reincarnation of David Lean by way of Stanley Kubrick.

That's when I heard a voice from another room."What is that music? It's BEAUTIFUL!"

My fiancée.

Now, my preference when in an altered state of consciousness is to be left alone with my thoughts... especially since, once I have eaten a pot brownie, I usually undergo a physical transformation and become a very shy and slovenly giant panda.

However, I was so shocked by my non-genre-fan-wife-to-be's very honest and visceral reaction to Goldsmith's music that, when she came into the room and sat next to me - telling me that she had never seen *TMP* - I not only welcomed her to join me in my ursine state, but also did nothing to warn her of what was to come.

What followed was, at the very least, the most fun viewing of *TMP* that I have ever experienced.

Watching this film in a high-definition display with an upscaling DVD player, my fiancee and I were struck by several things. One, most of the cast was in dire need of dance belts. The far-too-tight and pajama-like uniforms provide way more shapes, outlines, and suspicious shadows than a general audience should have to see.

Two, the make-up in this film was clearly not designed for the level of scrutiny possible in the digital viewing environment. In a 1080p presentation, most of the cast members - especially Spock - come across as spackled, painted, shellacked, and... a bit... well... for lack of a better word... queeny.

This may sound harsh, but once someone has pointed out to you that Leonard Nimoy's Spock make-up makes him look more like Faye Dunaway in *Mommie Dearest* than the incarnation of the character seen in the original TV series, it becomes extremely hard to see anything else.

Three, while we are on the topic of High Camp and melodrama - the film is so full of earnest and loudly declaimed declarations of shoulder-clutching masculine affection ("Dammit, Bones... I NEED you! BADLY!") that, especially in light of the first two items on this list, it is nigh-impossible not to project on the narrative a homoerotic subtext so overwhelming that I began to wonder whether Gore Vidal was hired to do a script rewrite and made trolling the hetero establishment his mission (as he famously admitted to doing with William Wyler's *Ben-Hur*).

These three factors taken into account, *Star Trek: The Motion Picture* rapidly became for us a Douglas Sirkian fever-dream *telenovela* in which Admiral Kirk once had love affairs - and amicable breakups - with Scotty, Sulu, Chekhov, McCoy, and Spock, but Kirk's most recent lover, Commander Decker, knew nothing of it until the Admiral's arrival on the *Enterprise* causing much hissing and rending of garments among all involved.

If you ever find yourself stoned out of your ever-loving capacity for reason - and in need of an evening of freely-interpretative reconsideration of an antiquated film - try watching *TMP* under this assumption. Every one of Spock's eyebrow-cocking reactions - every long, pining look between these heavily made-up, tightly pant-suited men - and every physical instance of manly fellowship will blossom into a previously undiscovered country of Mattachine passion.

All of which, I hope, proves beyond a shadow of a doubt that *Star Trek: The Motion Picture* is not only easy to mock... it may even actively reward mockery.

While I remember that night as a pivotal moment of bonding between me and my now-wife - and the impressions I relayed above are a reliable part of my comedic repertoire - the inciting incident for it remains etched in my memory and is the cornerstone of my increasing affection for *TMP*... my wife's reaction to Jerry Goldsmith's overture: "It's BEAUTIFUL."

In the thirty-eight years since the release of *TMP*, there have been five additional films starring the original cast, five television series set in the *Star Trek* universe, three feature film sequels to *The Next Generation* television series, and three films set in the "Kelvin Timeline" (the name given by Paramount Studios to the alternate universe established by J.J. Abrams and company in their 2009 reboot of the *Star Trek* franchise).

Not one of them has made me believe that there is beauty in the *Star Trek* universe.

All these different *Star Trek*s reflect their respective times, and the evolution of the mainstream of taste in popular entertainment: a taste which, in many ways (not the least of which is in the portrayal of ethnically-diverse casts and characters), *Star Trek* has helped define. However, one franchise alone, no matter how popular and pervasive - and how noble its aims - cannot remain static in the face of taste and culture.

In the past thirty-seven years, *Star Trek* has become as jacked-up, blown-up, and turned-up as every other popular entertainment (something I began to notice around the time someone decided that *Star Trek: Nemesis* needed to bring some much-needed off-road ATV racing to the franchise). While I have as much of a desire to have my senses overloaded by entertainment that is jacked-up, blown-up, and turned-up as the next guy, the word "beautiful" is seldom the one that comes up in apropos of entertainment that is jacked-up, blown-up, and turned-up.

In the time since that fateful night with the wife and the marijuana brownie, I have periodically revisited

TMP with newfound and growing affection for a number of reasons. None of them are drug-related. One is that its slow, stately pace does, in fact, allow the viewer to appreciate a great number of moments of artistry that are, inarguably, beautiful.

First and foremost there is Jerry Goldsmith's Academy Award-nominated score. While writing a defense of Jerry Goldsmith is like writing an apology for oxygen - simultaneously obvious yet well out of my weight category - I will say this: listening to Goldsmith, I always get the sense that I'm in the hands of a composer who could easily write John Williams as well as John Williams, but chose not to for the sake of having bigger fish to fry.

Don't believe me? Listen to the "The Calling/The Neigborhood" - the second track of the soundtrack for *Poltergeist* (a film regarded by most genre lovers as the evil, and significantly more entertaining, twin of Spielberg's *E.T.*). In less than five minutes, Goldsmith - with the steady and unpretentious hand of a prolific craftsman who habitually forgets more moves than comprise the repertoire of his peers - pastiches, parodies, and then out-Williams Williams before propelling himself into a sonic universe of his own invention.

For *TMP*, Goldsmith not only brought his mainstream Hollywood A-game (rightfully influenced by Williams' genre-defining work on *Star Wars* as well as Maurice Jarre in his sweepingest *Lawrence of Arabia* idiom) but also the experimental side that led him to pioneering work on films such as *Planet of the Apes, The Omen* and *Alien*; some of the first mainstream films to feature not only ethnic instruments and percussion, but also avant-garde influenced choral work, and electronic experimentation in concert with traditional orchestral techniques.

Like so much of what is artistically great about *Star Trek* in general, Goldsmith's score for *TMP* is often given short shrift simply because it exists in service of a science fiction franchise from the time before geek became chic - and because his main theme went on to become (in a sped-up and abridged version) the title music for all *Star Trek* for the next twenty years. If nothing else I write here compels you to revisit this film, consider spending two minutes and change listening to the <u>overture</u> alone.

If you don't find yourself agreeing with my wife, there is a strong chance you do not have a soul.

It is now a little-known fact that *TMP* was the most expensive studio film made for its time. Of course, if mere expense were the benchmark of a great film, then *Pirates of the Caribbean 4: On Stranger Tides* would be ranked well above *Citizen Kane* by the AFI. However, in the case of *Star Trek: The Motion Picture*, the studio's vast expenditure of production resources led to the creation of a richly detailed science fiction universe; one that was already years in development, as *TMP* was upgraded to movie status during a time when Gene Roddenberry had already spent a significant amount of time and money developing its foundations for a spinoff of the original *Star Trek* television series for a proposed fourth television network under the Paramount aegis.

At a time when films like *Star Wars, Silent Running*, and *Alien* were busily moving the needle of science fiction production design toward a workmanlike, junkyardy aesthetic that presented the future (or the past, in the case of *Star Wars*) as shopworn and kludged together over generations, *TMP* presented an almost final gasp of the sleek, inherently optimistic, mid-century modern future foreseen in films like *2001: A Space Odyssey* and the seminal

Forbidden Planet.

For better and worse, *TMP* is the most fully-realized, most epic version ever put on film of this "starship-as-mid-century-modern-hotel" aesthetic. In this respect, *TMP* is unmatched even by the many *Star Treks* that would succeed it, since by the time the studio got around to making *Star Trek II: The Wrath of Khan*, newly-installed director Nicholas Meyer made the decision - for reasons both aesthetic, and due to budget cuts made due to the bloat of *TMP* - to revamp the *Star Trek* universe with a gritty nautical flair inspired by World War Two submarine thrillers and the novels of C.S. Forester.

When Paramount Pictures greenlit *TMP*, the thinking behind the decision was extremely simple. George Lucas had just made enough money to purchase his own personal Endor with *Star Wars*: surely there was something in the studio's closet that could be quickly dusted off to not only compete, but also cash in on what studio heads must have then perceived as a fad with a limited window of opportunity. Today - when eighteen of the top twenty highest-grossing films of all time are science-fiction and fantasy (or some hybrid thereof) - it is hard to imagine a time when genre was so disreputable. In 1977, however, *Star Wars* was very much an outlier, and so, every effort had to be made to ensure that *TMP* was a "classy" production, a mainstream film with broad appeal beyond the Great Unwashed that once flooded NBC with letters for their beloved franchise's third-season renewal.

The choice of director Robert Wise, then, makes complete and perfect sense. A seasoned studio artisan and multiple Academy Award winner for classic films such as *West Side Story*, and *The Sound of Music*, Wise was also a genre adept whose films *The Day The Earth Stood Still*,

The Haunting, and *The Andromeda Strain*, achieved popular
success as well as good regard from the sci-fi, fantasy,
and horror faithful. Oh yeah, and there's also the fact that
he earned his first Oscar nomination for editing *Citizen
freakin' Kane*.

In hindsight, however, the hiring of Wise feels a
little tone deaf, considering that the goal was to drift off
the success of *Star Wars*. While Wise was (and I'll fight
anyone who says otherwise) a true artist of unimpeachable
accomplishment - indeed, one of the finest directors ever
produced by the Hollywood studio establishment - he
was pretty much the antithesis of the young soul rebels
who made *Star Wars*. Again, Lucas's methods may be
the establishment now, but in the late 70s, his grainy,
frenetically-edited, captured-in-documentary-style, and
grittily-designed universe was part of the late stage of a
revolutionary movement in independent, personal film
making, and Robert Wise was as far from that vanguard as
they got.

Of course, one might also argue that it was tone
deaf to set up *Star Trek* as a competitor to *Star Wars* in
the first place - especially in the marketplace of popular
entertainment. Whereas *Star Wars* was a pulp-action
fantasy space opera full of swashbuckling action, *Star
Trek* had always been more interested in intellectual
concerns, moral dilemmas, and utopian futurism... with
the occasional concession to military SF. While Paramount
certainly got a glossy and respectable Big Budget Studio
epic from Robert Wise, they sure as Surak didn't get *Star
Wars*... and we're all the better for it.

Regardless of the reception *TMP* received in 1979
(initial commercial success eventually limited by
critical disapproval), viewed outside of the commercial

considerations of its time, the film serves as a fascinating bridge between Hollywood's classical era and the then-dawning age of the modern tentpole blockbuster. It is hard to imagine that there was a time when a franchise that still exists today was being directed by someone who worked on *Citizen Kane*.

Working in a widescreen format that was already falling out of fashion in mainstream film - but which was back then synonymous with Old School Hollywood Spectacles, like Bible epics and war movies - Wise shows himself every bit the master of the *mise-en-scene* style of filmmaking. Like Orson Welles before him, Wise blocks his scenes in concert with the movement of the camera to create strong, pictorial frames in which cuts take place because they are motivated by the movement of the camera, which is in turn motivated by the movement of the actors, which is in turn motivated by the dramatic movement of the scene.

Where the dominant methodology in making today's films - especially major studio tentpole releases - is to secure as much "coverage" as possible (to shoot scenes from as many angles as possible) and then "find" the shape of the scene in the editing room, *mise-en-scene* work requires that a director make strong choices about the final look of the scene on the set. Coverage-based filmmaking allows greater flexibility after the fact to alter the pace, tone, and sometimes even the core story of a film, (something extremely useful in a marketplace in which films are test-screened and reshot multiple times in order to deliver to the audience the most satisfying experience possible). *Mise-en-scene* filmmaking generally requires a director to treat the script as final and plan accordingly - a dicey proposition in a film like *TMP*, which was rewritten so frequently through the course of its legendarily troubled production that script revisions arrived on the set not just with date stamps, but also hour stamps.

As a result, *TMP* may not always be the most gracefully written narrative, but, under Robert Wise's direction, it most certainly is a collection of elegantly choreographed picture frames depicting a wholly-designed artificial world. The camera moves when it has to, because it is motivated to do so by the action in the frame, and when it does, it is stately, like the *Enterprise* itself.

Working in this style, Wise forces himself to put all of his ingenuity toward the creation of painterly images with multiple levels of interest. Wise's frequent use of the split-diopter lens to create these frames is one of the most fascinating aspects of *TMP* as a master class in blocking and shooting scenes. The split-diopter allows multiple areas of the frame to stay in focus simultaneously, allowing for a tremendous amount of depth of field so that action can take place simultaneously over multiple planes without cutting away: the result often resembles an Old Master painting, with the deep focus capturing action and presenting story information on multiple levels from the extreme foreground to the far back.

By using this, and many other techniques - and choreographing his scenes with exquisite skill - Wise turns the *Enterprise* into a living, dynamic space without resorting to excessive camera movement or too accelerated an editing pattern: proving that "you are there" isn't merely a description that applies to the more modern, documentary-inspired style of directors like Paul Greengrass, or J.J. Abrams for that matter. While many fine directors have had their hand at putting the *Star Trek*

Universe on film, few have done so with the artistic rigor and commitment to style shown by Robert Wise, and allowed by *TMP*'s massive budget and resources.

I say this because artistic rigor and commitment to an aesthetic are qualities that have become very fluid in today's digitally-enhanced filmmaking: the flexibility (and cost savings) provided by shooting on digital media instead of costly film, as well as the infinite choices presented by non-linear editing, has made the process of putting together a film malleable long past the release date. One of the hallmarks of coverage-driven filmmaking is the overuse of close-up shots: both to punch up the emotional content of a scene, but also to cover up discrepancies in the position of the actors in the scenes because the flow and blocking of the scene has been altered in the editing. While Wise uses close-ups - what director doesn't? - he favors carefully positioned shots of multiple actors in various places in the frame when he cuts deeper into the scene from his master shot, selling the emotion of the moment not just by the intensity of the shot selection, but because the audience gets to watch the performers relate to - and build on - each other's work.

Because of Wise's directing style, the viewer of *TMP* gets to live in the *Enterprise*, and observe it - and the characters and their relationships, both emotional and spatial - in detail. While the film's admittedly slow pace may lead some viewers to wonder just HOW long they have to do this - to me, this style is something of a tonic in that it creates a mood and movement that feels organic to the type of story being told.

Like so much of the film's high-minded and idea-driven content, Wise's shooting style and scene design offers the space to appreciate not just the tale being told, and the sum of every artistic discipline that integrates into the greater whole of that story, but also the notion that this is a story about ideas, discovery, and the evolution of a soul... subjects which do not necessarily scream to be explored via hyperkinetic editing, a camera that moves as if wielded by a meth lemur, endless and massive close-up shots of actors, and scenes in which it is impossible to tell exactly where in the setting the characters began and ended.

So while Robert Wise may not have delivered a *Star Wars* competitor, he certainly delivered a *Star Trek* motion picture... and in delivering a *Star Trek* motion picture, Wise and his collaborators also delivered something that is redeemed from many of its considerable shortcomings by virtue of being magisterial, cinematic, thoughtful, and, again, occasionally, quite beautiful.

That much said, among all this beauty there are vast, heaping dollops of creamy yellow cheese... and there is one specific moment that encompasses all that is wincingly risible in Gene Roddenberry's hippy-dippy, utopian, up-with-people futurism - and his writing collaborators' ponderous groping toward rendering it as drama, and the huge amount of unintended homoerotic subtext, and the actors' often clumsy attempts to inhabit as middle-aged men roles they had not played in over a decade - and Robert Wise's attempts to wrap all of this in the bow of a major studio prestige release... all the while simultaneously embodying everything that is beautiful and worthwhile about *Star Trek*.

Recovering in sickbay after mind melding with "Vejur" - the massive and god-like creature of pure logic that is the film's main antagonist - Spock recognizes it to be barren of emotion. Finally realizing that his individual quest to rid himself of his own emotions in exchange for perfect logic is an evolutionary dead-end - because it ignores the wisdom, and hope, that is gained from an appreciation of everything that is imperfect - Spock takes Kirk's hand and passionately declares that... "Jim, this simple *feeling* is beyond Vejur's comprehension."

It can be difficult to love *Star Trek* as a fan. It has existed only slightly longer than I have, and as a result is a contemporary whose own maturation has been as rocky, embarrassing as that of any other adult: oftentimes moreso because it has always tried, and frequently failed, to appeal to whatever has been commercial in its time, and because it is not a creation that stems from a single source of monolithic ideas, but a colloquium of individuals - all trying to interpret Gene Roddenberry's vision for their own time.

Star Trek can be many things, but as *TMP* shows us so well, often times those things include overwhelming amounts of "dated," and "cringeworthy."

You can call me an old fuddy-duddy for saying this - and, please know that I have tried my level best to keep this from being a "they don't make 'em like they used to" rant, because... well, a lot of the time they <u>really</u> shouldn't - but one of the things *TMP* has taught me over the years is that I *like* my *Star Trek* a little heady... and ponderous... and willing to walk the line between post-graduate smart and stoner-tedious by tackling science-fictional concerns like the emergence of a god-like consciousness that does not understand the value of life with all of its flaws and foibles.

While *Star Trek* has never been a stranger to thrilling militaristic stories, and the sort of "us vs them" conflicts that are solvable with the application of force and sacrifice of lives, it has always attempted to wrap these, and all of its many stories, around an interrogation of the inscrutability - and essential necessity - of that "simple human feeling" that Spock so poignantly discusses with his friend during the climax of *TMP*.

There are many reasons to show sympathy for The Motion Sickness. There are also an equal number of reasons to laugh at its excesses, incongruities, and fumbles... but Spock's epiphany is the grand summation that makes the entire enterprise worthwhile. *Star Trek: The Motion Picture* is a film of bad decisions - brought into the world by faulty logic - that somehow, through the combined talent of every artist tasked with its creation, overcomes the faulty logic behind its own creation by being a beautiful monument to the very value of faulty logic.

Star Trek: The Motion Picture defies every edict to entertain in the same way as the films with which it was supposed to compete: instead, it takes its time with long takes, musical interludes, beautifully choreographed master shots, and plenty of meaningful pauses between emotive bursts of high declamation. *Star Trek: The Motion Picture* shows you its science-fictional world, not by dropping you into the action with the fast-cutting, middle-of-the-action, you-are-there-documentary-style immediacy of the first fifteen minutes of *Star Wars*, but with a slow-burn ponderousness that feels not just hopelessly dated, but also clumsily out of step with its own origin as televised pulp entertainment. *Star Trek: The Motion Picture* is a film that - almost defiantly - flaunts its many contradictions and inadequacies as if they were poetry... and then uses all of those contradictions and inadequacies to present a single idea that seems galactically silly at first... ... but which somehow lingers in the mind in the years that follow, and ultimately unfolds into a touching human truth.

And, in the end, what is the true measure of a movie's - any movie's - success? Is it aesthetic accomplishment and artistic perfection... or can success merely be that the work finds something reasonably novel to say about the common coin of our shared humanity? The latter is a simple, yet infinitely complex reason to love a flawed film, and yet, every time I watch *Star Trek: The Motion Picture* I find myself wondering how much better so many other films - many of them far more perfect and artistically accomplished - would be if they just made an effort to understand a concept so universal, yet fleeting, that even a character as wise, learned, and iconic as Mister Spock can only describe it as a "simple feeling."

THE ELEVEN LAWS OF SHOWRUNNING

Javier Grillo-Marxuach
1.20.16

INTRODUCTION AND APOLOGY

My friend John and I talk daily during my morning commute, which - over more than fifteen years, and regardless of what show I am working on that season - usually coincides with his lunch hour.

John and I have known each other since the sixth grade. Over the years, we have forged a close bond of friendship that transcends the distance between Los Angeles and our hometown of Ann Arbor, Michigan, where he still lives and works in the financial services industry.

There are many recurring topics in our ongoing conversation. Why were The Fixx always so much better live than in the studio and how weird that is for a synth pop band (or *were* they)? Why don't the people who play fantasy sports feel the same kind of persecution as those who play fantasy role playing games (I mean, they're pretty much the same damn thing)? Did Julian Fellowes actually hate Lady Edith and want her to suffer, or was his favoring of Lady Mary the result of an unexamined masochistic attraction to mean girls? Is a strong sense of empathy the thing that has kept us each from succeeding to the degree we wanted at this point in our lives? Are our respective addictions to to *Star Wars* Expanded Universe Novels and pulp books about barbarians a sign of emotional immaturity... or emotional strength?

Occasionally we talk about work.

Invariably, whenever I tell him some horror story about how the TV industry is run and the kind of... ahem... "colorful" bosses I have suffered with a stiff upper lip over the years, John concludes with the same statement: "I just don't understand how your business *works*."

After working on this document on and off for several of those years, I asked John to read it and give me his thoughts. He surprised me by telling me that he did not think I should publish it. When I asked him why, he further surprised me by saying that what I've written lacks empathy.

John's argument was that - though yes, I have worked for a lot of very unpleasant senior managers in my career - the tone of what follows is not merely angry, contemptuous, and merciless. In the following pages, John argues, I give no quarter to the possibility that all the bad behavior I'm calling out is the result of fundamentally human failings that perhaps are best addressed even-handedly: with the kindness that comes from writing calmly and dispassionately.

John also suggested that the following essay presents a side of me that is unlike the man he has been friends with for a very long time: a recovering Catholic turned foam-finger-and-body-painting-level fan of the New Testament who genuinely (if unevenly) aspires to take the High Road, forgive instead of avenge, and who truly believes in leading by example rather than force. That my best friend doesn't see that man in the pages that follow - and that it pains him to see me not just expressing myself, but also living with, such frustration and rage - certainly gave me pause and made me consider rewriting the whole damned thing.

I didn't.

Because I'm lazy? No. Because I'm vain? No. I mean, I probably am both those things, but they are not the reason I didn't junk the piece and start again with a more magnanimous frame of mind.

The reason is he's right. I am angry.

As we talked out his issues, I realized that, while John trying to protect me from showing the world my most vitriolic and judgmental side is the touching act of a true friend who does not want to see me judged by my behavior on my worst day, I <u>want</u> this rage to be heard.

I wrote this essay not caring if I'm seen as cranky, mean, and pissed, because - while I earn a good living being a good soldier to my employers - I'm not sure that my taking the High Road has done any good beyond earning me my pay and making sure whatever show I have been working on makes it out the door and into the airwaves.

Year after year - in a management culture that, on its best day, can't really be described as being particularly rigorous in the pursuit of professionalism - all I hear are more stories of escalating bad behavior, and I wonder: what would it take to better educate the rising class of showrunners?

My favorite scene in the history of television is in an episode of *The Sopranos*. Carmela visits an elderly Jewish psychotherapist. After patiently listening to her story, the therapist makes it clear that he thinks her husband is an evil man. The therapist judges Carmela: he knows that she is too lazy and comfortable with Tony's corruption to leave him. The therapist then refuses to take Carmela's money for the session because it gives him the right to tell her that now "you can't say that you were never told."

It is for that reason alone that I am letting fury have the hour.

In spite of my best friend's belief that I am putting something negative out into the world, I want it understood that bad leadership - even in a business concerned with things as trivial as telling nice stories to help people while away the time - has consequences.

Bad leadership perpetuates a cycle of incompetence, rage, and abuse. Bad leadership <u>makes good men cruel</u>.

If you're an aspiring writer who someday hopes to run the show, or if you are reading this because you sold a pilot and are curious about what a grizzled veteran - the kind you might be hiring as a co-executive producer - might have to say about it, then brace yourself... not for the snark and bile, but for this: you may find yourself tempted to behave poorly when your time comes, but after reading this, you will no longer be able to plead ignorance and innocence.

Now you can't say that you were never told.

PREFACE AND FURTHER APOLOGY

Upon finding this essay, any number of showrunners with whom I have worked in the past will assume it is a calculated personal attack: a retroactive shiv to the kidneys delivered in the language of a management lesson.

No matter that what follows is a distillation of some twenty years of experience - ten spent exclusively in upper-tier positions in television series - I wholly expect to read this by the light of bridges set on fire by any number of former bosses who will no doubt believe I am writing this out of envy, or to avenge some perceived slight, or was just too chickenshit to say it to their faces.

Also - and I'm just saying this to save obsessed fans the time and effort - there's nothing in the following 20,000 words about *Lost*.

If I have worked for you in the past and - after reading all these disclaimers - you still think that something in the following text is a singular attack on you, there's a song from the 1970s I'd like to play for you.

Carly Simon's lyrical stylings aside, it often takes that level of it's-all-about-me ego to be a television writer/producer: the conviction that what you have to say matters so much that it is worth not only mastering the tropes of an entire medium, but also the risk that all the intermediaries required to turn your interpretation of those tropes into the finished product (the actors, directors, producers, the person who embroiders the series logo on the back of the chairs) will ruin it all with some fatal blend of incompetence and incomprehension, or out of a calculating Salierian malice born from resentment of your undeniable genius.

The dark side of the drive to prove one's primacy of vision (colloquially better known as "I'LL SHOW YOU DADDY THAT YOU WERE WRONG TO NOT LOVE ME!") is that inefficient and self-indulgent - and more often than not abusive - senior management is endemic to the television industry. As cable, streaming, and Internet services adopt the television production model to generate content, the problem only gets worse.

Historically, there never was much of an apprenticeship/mentorship mentality in television - writers are notoriously taciturn and parochial about their "creative process." However, when there were only three to five broadcast networks and a much longer queue to the top of the food chain, someone who worked their way up the hierarchy from staff writer (the lowest and least paid position) to show creator/executive producer/ showrunner could at least be reliably understood to have at least spent a decade learning how to make the trains run on time under the oftentimes capricious tutelage of writer/ producers who had endured the same trials.

Nowadays, programming outlets are as likely (if not more, due to the never-ending quest for "a fresh voice") to buy television pilots from playwrights, screenwriters (many of whom toil for years - and are very well paid - without ever having to do the practical work involved in production), novelists, investigative journalists, and bloggers whose "my year of doing this and not that" article managed to break the Internet... and then put them in the position of having to manage what is essentially a start-up corporation with a budget in the eight figures and a hundred-plus employee workforce.

For many, the undeniable triumph that is pitching a series idea, having a pilot ordered, successfully producing it, and then having it ordered to series is nothing less than a validation: not only of their voice and talent, but also of their Way of Doing Things. This often translates to an intractable adherence to the notion that "my creative process" is so of the essence to success that all other concerns must be made subordinate lest the delicate alchemy that made success possible be snuffed.

The manager of a TV mogul whose work I guarantee you know and admire once encapsulated this to me with a story. Upon receiving his first series order, the then-neophyte showrunner declared "Good, I can now be the monster I always knew I could be."

This fundamental misunderstanding of what it means to be a showrunner is tacitly enabled by television networks and studios. The economics of TV and film are such that a single, long-running hit show can not only support entire multinational corporations, it also funds all of their development for years running. For a television network, a single tentpole series can cement the network's brand for decades to come, set the pattern for duplicatable success, and create enough wealth to make Midas blush.

Consider *CSI: Crime Scene Investigation*. For a decade-and-a-half, the *CSI* franchise anchored CBS's reputation as the go-to destination for solidly-crafted, edgy, visually-innovative, case-of-the-week crime procedurals. *CSI* set the pattern for the network's subsequent hit shows - most of them following the basic outline of a gifted investigator leading a team of specialists in solving exotic mysteries (*Without a Trace, Cold Case, Criminal Minds, Criminals Minds Beyond Borders, Criminal Minds: Suspect Behavior, NCIS, NCIS: LA, NCIS: New Orleans, Elementary, Limitless, Hawaii 5-0, Scorpion*). *CSI* also spun off three satellite shows (*CSI: Miami, CSI: NY*, and *CSI: Cyber*) - of which *Miami* surpassed even the original as the most watched television series in the world.

Most importantly - far more so than such esoteric concerns as "aesthetics" and "artistic accomplishment" - the sheer volume of revenue generated by *CSI* simply boggles any ordinary mortal's dreams of avarice.

With all of this at stake - with success literally meaning the difference between a fifteen-year bull market and a Saharan drought - is it surprising that most showrunners are, and are allowed to remain, some of the most incompetent senior managers in the business world?

Because a hit show has such revenue and image-generating potential, is it shocking that studios and networks will tolerate an almost endless amount of dysfunction - and are more than willing to avert their eyes from How The Sausage Is Made - in the name of getting it on time and on budget, and to preserve whatever sorcery it took to get there?

Of course not.

There are only two real sins for which a showrunner pays with a pink slip: wasting time and squandering money, and both of these contingencies are amply prepared for in studio plans and budgets. Missing an airdate and going egregiously (and I do mean "way beyond the pale" egregiously) over budget are the only two real firing offenses in the TV business... and, in truth, there is an entire army of dedicated professionals who stand beneath the showrunner day in and out to make sure that doesn't happen.

Why? Because they depend on the show - and the perceived creative and managerial genius of the showrunner - for their living. That's why.

So, once they have a show on the air, even the most inept of managers - or the most sociopathic of abusers - muddle through and keep their show on the air on something resembling time and on budget: usually by the sweat of a lot of talented individuals who are then denied credit for their toil at the altar of the "visionary auteur's" brilliance.

Beyond that, whose business is it if the writers are made to sleep in cots in their offices and only go home for showers because the showrunner can't decide what story is he or she wants to tell and has them rewriting scenes that shoot the next day while they create story for an episode that is already in prep and starts filming the day after but doesn't have a script yet? Or that the assistants are verbally abused on a daily basis because they can't cover the phones and pick up lunches while performing personal services such as taking the showrunner's medical samples to his doctor, shuttling his children to school and taping their recitals? Or that members of the art department are being asked by the showrunner's wife to redecorate their house and they are doing it because they know that to say no means to lose their job?

In the ultimate cost-benefit analysis, studios and networks quite simply do better letting their precious messianic autocrats persist in their belief that they are geniuses on par with Mozart - and that it is only the sheer idiosyncrasy of their "creative process" that allows the show to go on - than to take the risk of disrupting the creation of a hit show with such earthly concerns as fomenting a workflow that actually takes into account that the employees are human beings.

As long as the show comes in on time, on budget, and makes money, most showrunners quite simply have complete authority over the internal management of their operation.

The dirty little secret of TV, however, is that those who get their pilots made and show picked up on any given year are usually no more gifted, visionary, or prodigious, than the ones who did not. There are as many television writers who work regularly as there are professional NBA players at any given time - and, by that metric, we are all breathing rarefied air - but the process by which television shows are made and selected is by no means some mystical divination by which the special artistry of very special snowflakes is empowered that it may elevate the art form as a whole.

This is what actually happened when a show got on the air: an inventor (I mean "a writer") had an idea. Through a series of channels ("agents") the inventor went to a venture capitalist ("a studio") and got some guidance about developing the product. Together they then took it to a retailer ("network") who agreed to front money to build a prototype ("pilot"), and later, based on that prototype and their extant successes and projected needs (the "shows that they kept from last year and the ones that got cancelled"), they decided to put the entire product line (the "series") in their department store windows (their "air").

Television is - quite simply - a business: with seasonal patterns, production schedules, budgets, and deliverables... just like any other business.

And that's the dirtiest secret of the trade: it ain't magic, it ain't alchemy, and it sure as Shinola ain't mystical. The critics may call this a "golden age" - and it very well may be - but it's not the work of druidic conjurers on exotic hallucinogens wresting narrative from altars of living rock.

What we do is nothing more - or less - than mere hard work... hard work that is not exclusive to any one person, but helped along by scores of competent, experienced professionals whose job security is tied to the longevity of the endeavor... hard work that can be done efficiently and thoughtfully... hard work that can be accomplished in a way that doesn't ask anyone involved to sacrifice their lives, dignity, and - sometimes - personal safety.

As special and wonderful as creativity may be, it is something that can be channeled, managed, made to work on call, and sent to bed at a decent hour. Any television show - from the worst of the formulaic, to the most genre-defining, medium-transforming phenomenon - can be made on time, on budget, and without demanding that any of the employees put more time at the mine than they absolutely have to... if the showrunners simply apply basic, commonsensical management strategy to their creative process.

Though specific to the day-to-day workflow of television, and the issues of writing and producing episodes of a series week in and week out, the following "laws" will seem - in principle - bafflingly simple to anyone who has worked in a professional environment, understands the need to effectively communicate to employees the goals of an organization in order to succeed, and believes that effective leadership comes from giving clear commands and directives. Yet the truth remains that the number of showrunners whose staffs would describe them as "effective managers of the creative process" is in the minority.

Why is it so hard to implement some simple strategies in the name of running the show more efficiently?

The simple answer is that "simple" doesn't necessarily mean "easy." In my experience, the simplest decisions are often the hardest because they demand a painful concession to an unpleasant truth. In the case of every one of the laws hereafter, they all ask for the same thing: that a showrunner surrender some infinitesimal quantum of their ego - of their attachment to the idea of themselves as the sole fountainhead of creative greatness - to serve the show and those who work to make it instead of themselves.

It seems like a contradiction - to ask someone from whom visionary leadership is demanded to surrender their ego - but it isn't, because of...

THE FIRST LAW OF SHOWRUNNING
IT'S ALL ABOUT YOU
STOP MAKING IT ALL ABOUT YOU

Seriously. It REALLY is all about you.

You pitched an idea, sold a script, and got it made. You did it. You pushed it past the *pezzonovanti.* Now you have sixty million dollars and thirteen hours of network airtime - with a strong possibility for much more - for a bully pulpit. Nothing goes in front of the lens that you do not approve. Nothing gets on the screen without your stamp.

So you finally have the Brass Ring... and guess what? It won't make that you never found a publisher for your first novel any less painful, and it won't make your daddy finally love you, or your spouse more sexually compliant, or your kids less disdainful of your bad puns and clumsy attempts to make them understand that you really DID like and understand that last Sky Ferreira album.

You're still you. All the shit you hate about yourself is never going away. Deal with that.

And let me make one thing clear about the motif of "daddy issues" in this essay. I know the love of an effusive, demonstrative, and generous father - one whose accomplishments will forever dwarf mine, but never made our lives a competition - but I nevertheless have been made to suffer the madness, rage, and abuse of a cavalcade of bad mentors, bosses, and colleagues, male and female... many of whom I mistakenly looked to for professional and personal validation.

So, if you are already rearin' to say "Whew - none of this applies to me because I like my father," go ahead and choke on that. Everyone has some dominant figure in their lives that makes them feel worthless: I'm using "daddy" because, in this still male-dominated industry, it's often as prosaic as that. One recurring point in this is that the motivational influence of your personal demons diminishes far more rapidly than does their effect in making you the same as them to others. That's what "daddy" means to me.

So... now that it's finally all about you... you wanna know what it means? When it's all about you?

More work.

For a functional showrunner, "more work" translates into putting your affectations behind, and performing day-in-and-out in service of your vision and your staff. Once you accept that, accept this too: your staff works for you. They will do whatever you need done because they enter every conversation knowing that you can fire them. Their indenture is a given.

Their loyalty is not.

By and large, your staff is here for a paycheck - that and the dimly remembered hope that they will receive some sort of creative fulfillment in the plying of their craft. It's on you to invest them in the vision of the show and turn them into true believers and dedicated workers who will go the extra mile... you do that by giving them the opportunity to express themselves within the framework you have created.

You know how you DON'T do that? By continually - and either passive-aggressively, or aggressively-aggressively - reminding them who's boss.

Everyone. Knows. It. Already.

The real question is: What will you do with that power? Will you demand that everyone jockey for your favor in order to have the information they need to do their job, or will you provide the information freely so that creativity blooms because, and not in spite, of you?

Are you strong and secure enough in your talent and accomplishment to accept the possibility that other people - properly empowered by you - can actually enhance your genius... or will you cling to the idea that only you can be the source of that genius?

How you answer that question determines the leader you will be.

THE SECOND LAW OF SHOWRUNNING
KNOW YOUR SHOW
AND TELL EVERYONE WHAT IT IS

It seems weird that someone would sell a show and then not really "know" what it is - or would be unwilling to share that information. Kind of like Steve Jobs not telling his staff more about the iPhone than that "it makes calls"... and yet, not knowing - or not telling - what the show is, is one of the most common, and chronic, diseases of the incompetent showrunner.

You see, there's more to knowing your show than understanding why you feel bad about your daddy never loving you and that you were able to turn that set of emotions into a police procedural (though your writers will most likely need that information stated to them very clearly and frequently that they may understand what you want them to deliver). All of your employees - from the directors to the costume designers to the guy who embroiders the back of the chairs - need specific knowledge of the tone, texture, and technique of the show to do their jobs.

Even after producing the pilot episode, most of that valuable and absolutely crucial information still remains in

your head. Remember, the pilot episode was a prototype
- and was probably picked over by everyone at network,
studio, marketing, etc. Now you have to discern what it
was that worked so well in the pilot - and it may not have
been solely the parts you were able to dictate and control -
and turn them into a reproducible result. You also have to
figure out the things that didn't work - a task that requires
a certain amount of honesty and self-reflection - and then
articulate to your writers and your crew how you want
them fixed.

Regardless of what you have been told about sitting in
a garret and writing scripts that would make Rod Serling
turn green, most of your work as a showrunner is to
communicate that information to other people so that they
can execute it within their field of expertise.

One of the great contradictions of the way we make
television in the United States is that writers are given
managerial control over the entire enterprise... but writers
are very often by nature not very good communicators
outside the page. Also, talking to people non-stop, all day,
with great specificity, about a project this size, is hard, and
tiring. Easier to hide in your office and wait for them to
come to you, right?

Well... it is true that not everyone believes that
knowing what they want, and reaching out to those who
need to know it in order to perform, is a necessity for
success in the world of television... and this is the part
where they come out from their slimy, shit-stained hole
and excuse their lack of vision (or their unwillingness to
impart that vision) with a defense I consider to be the most
cowardly and thieving seven words in the showrunner's
lexicon: "I'll know it when I see it."

If you ever find yourself saying that, kindly consider

the possibility that - and I mean this, from the heart - your impostor syndrome is most likely real and you are, in fact, a shrill, shrieking fraud.

Here's what "I'll know it when I see it" means to me and to everyone who hears it from a showrunner: "I have no original ideas of my own but am perfectly willing to let everyone else spin their wheels and exhaust themselves emotionally and creatively so that I can eventually cherry-pick the best of their genius and claim it for my own."

The field of television is littered with the desiccated husks of eager artists of all stripes - from writers to casting directors, production designers, actors, scenic painters, set builders, and the people who embroider the backs of the chairs - who, in the name of their own honor and work ethic, wore themselves out on the wheel of "I'll know it when I see it"... and the high castles surrounding those fields are occupied by fat, bloated barons who sit on their comfy thrones wondering with great self-pity why they can't seem to hire a staff that just "gets it."

When you're a showrunner, it is on you to define the tone, the stakes, the story, and the characters. You are NOT a curator of other people's ideas. You are their inspiration, their motivator, and - ultimately - the person responsible for their implementation.

Bottom line: the creativity of your staff isn't for coming up with your shit for you, it's for making your shit bigger and better once you've come up with it!

To say "I'll know it when I see it" is to abdicate the hard work of creation while egotistically hoarding the authority to declare what is or isn't good. "I'll know it when I see it" is an act of intellectual theft on par with plagiarism.

Anyone can say "I'll know it when I see it." The

writer's ability to MAKE SHIT UP is the reason we, and not the producers or the directors, are the showrunners in American television. To be an effective showrunner, you have to articulate what Maya Lin once referred to as "a strong, clear vision." You have to draw the boundaries of the sandbox with extreme precision, detail, consistency, and integrity.

And you know what? That's hard. It requires intellectual and creative rigor, it requires a measure of non-solipsistic introspection, and it requires that you make a discipline out of talking to other people and being on message at all times.

You know what else? That's your job. Surprise!

Turns out showrunning isn't about sitting alone in a darkened office wrestling your personal demons until they come out on the page as genius. Your job is to communicate a shared vision with enough specificity that everyone understands it, and to then preach it, day in and out, to the point of exhaustion until everyone - from the directors to the actors to the guy who embroiders the back of the chairs - feels it in their soul like a gospel.

And here's the great part of successfully communicating a shared vision: your employees will love you for it.

You can give out jackets with the show's logo. You can send an ice cream truck to the set. You can hand out fifty-dollar bills to the assistants in penance for screaming obscenities at them. You can even – as I saw a showrunner do in a shocking act of condscension masquerading as motivational boosterism – print up a leaderboard and give away gold and silver stars for "good ideas"...

But that's just bread and circuses. That's bribes.

Loyalty to an employer begins with the knowledge

of what the job is. Loyalty comes from knowing that your bosses have your back both in the form of giving out the information necessary to not only do what you do and do it right, and also the empowerment to use your own creativity to try to improve on the baseline.

Loyalty is the product of knowing that the boss trusts you with the crown jewels.

And yes, that's a hard leap of faith for the showrunner to make. Luckily you're a visionary and not an "I'll know it when I see it" person.

Right?

As someone who has squandered hours, days, and weeks - and more than once, months - of his life in the vampiric feeding troughs of multiple "I'll know it when I see it" showrunners, I am not above hitting below the belt on this one...

Every time you say "I'll know it when I see it," <u>you're proving daddy right</u>.

<u>*THE THIRD LAW OF SHOWRUNNING*</u>
ALWAYS DESCRIBE A PATH TO SUCCESS

I know, I know... we're not even a third of the way there and already you have SUCH a headache... being a leader is so tough, and tedious, and you already feel high lonesome for the days when you were young and careless, and could stay up late in your home office, writing your precious little scripts in a nimbus of Red Bull, nicotine, and online porn.

I feel your pain, Sparky, but stick with me here. This one is directly related to the last and a real pattern emerges from here on out. I promise.

Describing a path to success is the natural outgrowth

of Know Your Show and Tell Everyone What It Is at All
Times. This piece of advice was given to me by the non-
writing Executive Producer on my show *The Middleman* - a
very seasoned production executive who strove to create
an environment where I could excel in communicating the
goals of the show to all comers. "Always Describe a Path
to Success" simply means - in its most practical form - "Do
not leave a meeting without letting everyone there know
what they are expected to do/deliver next."

The most toxic thing a showrunner can do before
leaving the writers room - or any room, for that matter - is
to say "fuck it, I don't know, guys, figure it out." Which is
like saying "I'm leaving it up to you losers to disappoint
me: go!"

If you tell your staff how to please you, two out of
three times they will come back with a way to do exactly
what you want. If they can't, they will often come up with
a number of better ideas than the one you pitched out of
a desire to address the spirit, if not the letter, of a clear
directive.

Every clear directive you issue is a gift to your staff
because it relieves them of the duty to go back into their
offices, slaughter a lamb, and read its entrails in the hopes
that a close examination of their arterial topography will
divinely reveal a portent indicating what the fuck it is that
you really want.

A clear directive is - once again - an indication of trust.
See the pattern emerging here? A clear directive is your
way of saying "Here's the hill we have to take. I have
taken the time and effort to figure out the goal. I now
acknowledge that you have the knowledge and resources
to figure out the strategy in a way I cannot."

To successfully define a path to success, you don't

even have to know the exact hill to take. The grinding race that is television often means that you yourself may not always know the next goal; but even if you articulate your order as "Help me figure out the next hill to take," or "Let me know what our resources are so that I can make an educated decision about which of all these hills we should attack next," that alone constitutes a directive with a defined outcome.

You will be amazed at how much even that measure of clarity will galvanize a team.

Your job as a showrunner, then, requires that you exert your creativity on the definition of the problems ahead. By doing that job - hard though it may be - what you are doing is to free your staff to do what they do best: dedicate their unique skills to their solution.

THE FOURTH LAW OF SHOWRUNNING
MAKE DECISIONS EARLY AND OFTEN

As the days, weeks, and months of pre-, pro-, and post-, churn away, you will find that - whether you like it or not, and whether it's in your comfort zone or not - everyone in your sphere constantly solicits decisions from you... and why shouldn't they? It's all about you, right?

And yet, an aversion to making decisions is a massively common ailment in the showrunning trade. As showrunner diseases go, decision aversion might as well be Non-Hodgkin's, Ebola, and the thing from Jerry's Kids all rolled up into one lethal, morale-destroying, confidence-eroding, life-sucking, uber-malady.

Decision-averse management is one of the many offshoots of "I'll know it when I see it"... but unlike its more deleterious cousin, it does come out of an understandable insecurity...

You see, once you make a decision, the world knows where you stand. Once you say "This is what this is," you have made your taste and opinion clear: and the world will judge you.

People will come out of the woodwork with their little notes, and their little suggestions, and their little ideas, and their little "improvements"... and because you are a socially awkward little writer who wants nothing more than to please daddy, you will feel the need to compromise... and then your vision will be diluted... and then the world will never know your genius.

Now, I may have said that this insecurity is "understandable." And it is. No one likes to be judged and no one likes to defend their taste: especially when you are already exposing to a national audience what is essentially a dramatic expression of your innermost feelings and desires transformed into a police procedural.

What I am also saying is that it's also bullshit of the highest order and conduct unbecoming a showrunner.

Of course, you will now attempt to rationalize your decision aversion as part of the magical process by which you weigh all the options until you happen on the best possible one.

Wrong. Your decision aversion is not proof of your intellectual rigor and uncompromising taste. By and large, and to the great exasperation of many a member of your staff, the option with which the decision-averse showrunner ultimately runs is usually, and most likely, among the first they are pitched.

No. Your decision aversion is a stalling tactic designed to let you have it your way without ruffling too many feathers because you are way too invested in being seen as a "nice person" and a "good boss."

But you know what "nice people" and "good bosses" actually do? They rip off the Band-Aid early, make the case for their decision, hear out any remaining arguments to a reasonable degree, then shut down the discussion and send everyone off to get on with their work.

Yup. That's what "nice" actually looks like: because while "nice" can mean "affable" and "pleasant," a second definition of "nice" is also "precise and demanding careful attention."

You want to be "nice?" That's the nice to strive for. You could also try and smile a little, Sparky - we've all seen your brand new Tesla on the lot and it's pretty fucking... nice.

Avoiding a decision until the last possible minute while everyone runs themselves ragged coming up with contingency after contingency? That's neither flavor of nice. That's you assuming no one will love you unless you keep them on the leash with the false hope that they may eventually get their way... it's keeping everyone attached from their lips to your buttocks until you finally deign to nut up and do the thing you were going to do anyway, because the show cannot go on until you say what the show is.

Your job is to make ideas come to life. The first step in doing your job is to commit. Commit early. Commit often. Make committing the same as breathing: you might as well do it now, because you will have to do it eventually.

Most importantly, the sooner you make a decision, the sooner you will know from your crew what is achievable, and the sooner they will be able to expand upon - and use their talents to elevate - it. The time you spent not deciding is time you rob from your staff's ability to make whatever the object of the decision the best it can be.

With alarming frequency, I see decision-averse showrunners look at dailies, or a director's cut, and say something like "Man, that set/costume/casting choice/ embroidery on the back of that chair sucks. Why does it suck?"

The answer is, invariably, "Oh, I dunno, Sparky, because you waited until the last minute to decide what you wanted and no one had the time to make it the best it could be?"

Of course, you can't say that because the showrunner suffering from this disease doesn't want to feel judged... the decision-averse showrunner wants to be told that there are no casualties in their perceived search for excellence, and that all would be fine if everyone else were just as rigorous and demanding in their own work.

Invariably, this leads to the eventual firing of the set/ costume designer/casting director/back of the chair embroidering guy. It's unfair, it sucks, and now that you have heard it from me, you can't pretend no one ever told you.

And as far as your desire to not be judged goes - toughen up, Sparky. Judgment - like winter - is coming. No matter what you do. Judgment is coming. It comes for the weak. It comes for the strong. It comes for the hacks and the geniuses in equal measure.

So do you want to go down swinging or do you want to go down like a chump?

Make that your first decision.

THE FIFTH LAW OF SHOWRUNNING
DO NOT DEMAND A FINAL PRODUCT AT THE IDEA STAGE

When you sold your pilot, you didn't take an eight-million-dollar film of your script to the network meeting with you. You talked the executives through your idea for a series, the characters, and your story for the pilot, and they proceeded to entrust you with millions of dollars to fulfill your vision.

Considering how much the creation of a TV series depends on a studio and network's ability to visualize a bunch of words on the page - or coming out of some writer's mouth - it is terrifying to me how many allegedly seasoned and experienced showrunners lack the simple skill to understand a story when it is pitched to them off note cards on a board.

Another example of this inability to visualize on the conceptual level has taken place on several shows I have worked on... shows in which the staff has had to write, and rewrite *ad nauseum,* thirty- to forty-page outlines including dialogue in order to convince the showrunner that - as members of the Writers Guild - we have the ability to render in script a scene that, on a note card on the board, or an outline, should be as simply stated as "they meet cute."(And, later - after micromanaging the concept phase to the exclusion of any and all invention on the part of the episode writer - the showrunners in every one of these shows have invariably had the audacity to complain that the final scripts with which they were presented lacked a certain... oh, I don't know... "flicker of inspiration" and were just "the outlines with more dialogue.")

Architects can see buildings off blueprints. That's their job. Your job as a showrunner is to see the gross anatomy of the stories the writers pitch you off the shorthand of the board, and to let them run with the details.

The next step is to visualize even further down the line as the writers refine the muscular, circulatory, and nervous systems in the slightly more detailed treatment of the story, plot, and scenes in an outline, and - if you don't like the shape of the surface once the script comes in - for you to give notes and rewrite if necessary.

If, as a showrunner, you repeatedly have to return stories to the board after they have been outlined or scripted for gross anatomy work - or find yourself sending your writers off to script and outline in frustration, only to then rewrite from page one – you may want to consider doing some work on your own ability to create and discern story from the foundations up.

Not all writers have this ability, but it is something that can and should be learned - and which is crucial to making television - because the physical production of the scripts depends on the departments having consistent, and accurate communication from the writers office as to what is coming down the pike.

Problem is, a lot of showrunners - especially those who do not come from television and did most of their gestational work alone and outside of the collaborative environment of the writers room - hate the writers room.

They hate the panoply of voices - and they hate having to occasionally quiet them for fear of being seen as "not a nice guy." They also hate the leap of faith that comes from hearing a story told to them in strokes bolder than the fine grain of a script - and they especially hate the subsequent leap of faith that the writers will render the story in a way that matches their voice exactly.

What a lot of these showrunners wind up doing is either protracting the story breaking process - asking for such detail in the story break that the writers room becomes a compulsive-obsessive death march that snuffs out all of the creativity that would eventually happen when the writer finally faces the blank page - or simply punting on the writers room altogether.

Many an incompetent showrunner simply retreats to a position where he or she accepts a story from the writers room only in the boldest of strokes - declaring approval in the same way a wild animal caught in a bear trap chews off its own arm in exchange for freedom - only to then rewrite everything from page one when the script comes in... again, to the detriment not just of the writers, who feel that they were sent off on a fool's errand, but also of all the people who need to know what's actually going to go in front of the camera in order build, produce, and rehearse it.

One of the things increasingly lost as showrunners are no longer asked to work their way up the ranks in the television hierarchy is a comfort level with collaboration in the form of the writers room, and a knowledge of story - usually born of coming up with one story after another on other people's shows. It is from this longitudinal experience of collaboration and story generation that most showrunners learn how to visualize from the blueprint level.

How, then, if you do not come from a lifetime of conference and teamwork, but find yourself forced into collusion with a writers room - whom you need, if for no other reason, to generate the sheer volume of material the show demands - do you develop this skill?

The answer is simple. Trust.

You trust that the extremely expensive staff of professionals you hired - and which the studio pays extremely well (some of them earn almost as much as you do!) - can actually... you know... write.

You trust that a writer who pitches you "meet cute" on a note card on the board can actually write a decent "meet cute" and doesn't have to act it our for you in the room - because, let's face it, few of us are actors and the room ain't exactly The Groundlings Theater.

Just like you, dear showrunner, other writers occasionally need to retire to their keyboards to do their job to the fullest - and because you will decide whether or not they have to be fired after they turn their draft, they are profoundly invested in doing a good job...

What you need to understand above all things when it comes to the writers room is that you are not "the audience": you are the "chief designer and architect." Sure, you can demand to be "entertained" by work that feels complete in its gestational phase, but know that the inevitable product of that demand is that you will be bored by it by the time it reaches your desk as a script because you will have effectively destroyed a crucial part of your staff's creative process...

And, ironically, it's the part of the process that most showrunners guard jealously for themselves...

THE SIXTH LAW OF SHOWRUNNING
WRITE AND REWRITE QUICKLY

Okay, Sparky - this one's gonna be harsh... so I'm gonna start by smearing Desitin on your ass, putting a fresh clean diaper on top, and telling you everything's going to be all right.

Yes, your scripts - as well as the ones you rescue from that nasty, overpaid and underachieving staff of writers who don't "get it" - are, in fact an expression of your fragile soul. That's right - and they must be protected at all cost from the judgments of all the bad people in the world who want to turn your special and precious little show into something vulgar and gaudy.

You know what else a script is? A work order.

Without a complete script, no one can decide where they are going to take the trucks with all the lights and cameras and costumes, and for how long. Without a script, no one can figure out how much it's going to cost to make this episode of your series. Without a script, the actors can't prepare themselves for their work in front of the camera.

A script is the final and most specific description of the work that is ahead of the production for several weeks to come. If you procrastinate - or hold your precious to your bosom like Gollum - NO. ONE. KNOWS. WHAT. THEIR. JOB. IS.

And there's someone else who needs to read your work on the page to understand their job. Your writers.

Think about it. A studio has given you millions of dollars to hire a large staff of people whose mission is to learn how to produce work that reads and sounds like your voice: the voice that you convinced a network and a studio was worth a loan in the tens of millions to realize a television series.

Reproducing that voice is a primary facet of your writing staff's work; the best and most efficient way they can do that is by reading your prose and dialogue. The faster you write and deliver material to your team, the sooner they can integrate your voice into the process... and the faster you rewrite their work, the faster they can internalize your changes to their work into the matrix of that learning process.

For most competent writers working under the

exigencies of a television season, a week and a half
is considered ample time to write the first draft of
a script from a solid story break and outline... and
yet, showrunners routinely avail themselves of an
unconscionable span of time to write their own scripts...
especially when that script is a tone-setting season
premiere.

On at least three different shows, I have spent some
eight weeks, along with the rest of the writing staff,
spinning our wheels trying to break story and create
further narrative, while waiting for the showrunner to
write a season premiere.

During that time, the show's writers are invariably
ordered by the showrunner to launch into their own scripts
(as studio, network, and production demand to know what
exactly is going on and why the pipeline isn't yielding
new material) and without fail, those scripts are eventually
judged as inferior in light of all the new "discoveries"
made by the showrunner during their lengthy retreat into
their "creative process" - a retreat for which everyone
winds up paying in time, wasted creative energy, and time-
filling busywork.

In one particularly catastrophic incident, the two-
hour season premiere of a major network series had to be,
almost literally, forcibly seized by the network president
after two months of the showrunner comma-fucking his
draft... only to be ultimately revealed as so unfilmably
divergent from what the showrunner had promised that it
had to be junked entirely.

A replacement two-hour season premiere had to
be written over the course of five business days and a
weekend by all the other writers on the staff, each taking
fifteen-page segments of the script. Once assembled,

the results were predictably patchy. The writers never recovered from the delay, the show never really found its voice, the season was poorly received, and the series never recovered.

In the other cases, the showrunners merely emerged from their cozy little garret after neglecting their writers room for weeks on end, only to deliver exactly the story that had been broken by the staff on the board, and then pitched to the network and studio, and outlined. Much to everyone's shock and horror, our leaders had availed themselves of two months to accomplish what we would all be expected to do in less than a week per writer per draft for the remainder of the year.

Yup. Real morale booster.

So here's the brass tacks, Sparky: your show's scripts, as written - or rewritten - by you, are your most effective tool in your performance of the Second Law. You can't talk to everyone at all times, and eventually, you have a responsibility to take your talk from the theoretical to the real.

That's what a script ultimately represents: the concretization of your voice and gesture. A script is the closest thing there can be to a finished product until you have a final cut. A script is your proof of concept, and if its fate is to fail that proof, then you are better off knowing sooner rather than later, so that you - and all of your employees - can use the time to fix what's broken and right the ship while there is still time.

Scripts are not just the cry of your wounded inner child - and those of the writers in your employ, by the way - but also the most crucial and efficient form of communication between cast, crew, studio, and network available to you. Write them quickly, rewrite them impassively and efficiently. Work your scripts until they are ready, but recognize that in a fast-moving business like television, most of the time they will only be ready enough.

Your best ideas will survive criticism; the worst ones... well, let's just say that there's no amount of parental attachment on your part that can keep them alive, and that it may not be worth fighting so hard for every single one of your precious children anyway, because the horizon is full of other children, all of whom need your immediate attention and will quickly make you forget the ones you've had to leave behind...

THE SEVENTH LAW OF SHOWRUNNING
TRACK MULTIPLE TARGETS EFFICIENTLY
BY DELEGATING RESPONSIBILITY

In the 1980s, the members of the Berlin Symphony told a joke about their notoriously imperious conductor, Herbert Von Karajan. It went like this: The *maestro* gets into a taxi. The driver asks "Where to?" "It doesn't matter," Von Karajan declaims, "I'm needed EVERYWHERE!"

With or without the colossal arrogance, that is one of the essential truths of showrunner life. This is why understanding the First Law, and practicing the Second, are so important. As the CEO of your own startup corporation, you are responsible for every facet of the production of your series: yes, even the embroidery on the back of the chairs.

And though the writers room - the forge of your show's creation - is the single most important place in the universe as far as you should be concerned, everything conspires to keep you away from it.

(Let me add here that if you don't think the writers

room is the single most important place in the world for you to be, you're wrong. Unless you're by nature a monomaniac, masochist, or misanthrope: the kind of insecure buffoon who needs constant proof that "no one gets it but me". You're not alone in this fallacy, however, and can have a long and storied career of making great television while avoiding the writers room and all those horrible little writers in it: those trolls who constantly debate everything until they choke the life out of it... mostly because you have taught them to behave that way by dint of never making a decision. One showrunner - another multiple award-winner whose work I guarantee you respect and admire - once told me in a meeting that "The writers room is where lazy people go to hide from real work." After I tried to divest him of this stupidity, he proceeded to not hire me and went on to win an Emmy. Go figure.)

At any given moment during the course of a standard television season, there are five stories that have to be minded: the story in development on the board in the writers room, the story in outline, the story being scripted, the story being shot, and the story being completed in editing and post-production.

That means meetings. Costume meetings, set decoration meetings, hair and make-up meetings, budget meetings, casting concept calls, network and studio notes calls on multiple drafts of multiple scripts, outlines, and stories, sound and special effects spotting in post-production... enough meetings to wear down even the most extroverted mass-communicator.

And yet, your job is to track all those targets. And never forget that to accurately and proactively communicate the theme, look, and style of your show

to all these people at all times is the Second Law of
Showrunning... but you do have a secret weapon in your
arsenal designed exactly to combat the fatigue that comes
from always having someone at your door who needs to
be told what is what.

That weapon is, of course, your writers.

It turns out that your writers are not, in fact, a
parliament of meanies whose job it is to take no end of
pleasure in getting your vision wrong on the page while
endlessly explaining to you in the room that your shit
stinks.

Though you don't realize it just yet, your writers are, in
fact, your <u>apostles.</u>

Yes... believe it or not, that motley and smelly bunch
of malcontents you keep trying to avoid is - in reality - a
misfit band of spiritual warriors ready to spread your
Evangel to every corner of your show's domain. Believe it
or not, that's their actual job!

The reason the ranking system of writers goes from
staff writer, to story editor, to executive story editor, to
co-producer, producer, supervising producer, and co-
executive producer, is because you're not just running
a show - you're also running a producer/showrunner
academy (and even if you are woefully uninterested in
teaching/under qualified to teach this discipline, this is the
duty that fate has thrust upon you).

The way you run a producer/showrunning academy
is by making the writers in the room the privileged bearers
of your knowledge of What the Show Is and then sending
them off to all these meetings to give voice to your unique
vision.

The reason the Second Law is so important is that, once
you use it to empower your people to spread the Word,

it actually takes stress and labor off your hands... I know, right?

Tracking multiple targets is difficult. Not just "whiny bitch" difficult, but actually physically and emotionally draining. It is a nigh-insurmountable, and ever-rising, Everest of work.

An exhausted showrunner - one who ran a show for over half a decade before handing it off for a run that continues to this day - once confided to me that "What they never tell you is that the job really is bigger than any one person". Not only is he spot on, but it is for that exact same reason that, over decades of television history, a system evolved by which a team of highly creative people were put in a privileged position of access to the seat of power and knowledge.

All you have to do is share with your writer/ producers/showrunners-in-training What You Want, then send them off to all the meetings, and have them report back... and here's the beauty part of all this: it's not as if you have to give up your command authority and surrender all of your ego, you only have to surrender a tiny little bit for a tiny little amount of time.

Remember the First Law, and remember that there will always be a final meeting on all these matters before the scenes are shot.

That's right, Sparky, you can always change your mind.

Why should you ask for help tracking multiple targets? Because it all begins with the story - that's why - and you need to focus your energy on making sure that the stories are developed to your satisfaction from the ground up.

The more your stories represent the purest version of your vision, the more involved will be your writers's knowledge of that vision... and the better your scripts are going to convey the vision to everyone else involved with the production (as well as the outlying regions, like the people who cut your promos at the network, or the people who license the show for merchandising).

And yes, I'm sorry to report that the process by which your stories portray your world view with great and specific passion and clarity happens in the place you hate most: the writers room.

Even if you successfully defeat your inner control freak and efficiently convey your message - and your writers carry it out without any signal degradation, and your orders are performed to the letter - you still have the daunting task of charting the creative course of a season that can span anywhere from ten to twenty-four episodes.

As I said at the beginning, that means you have some permutation of a story in development in the room, a story in outline, a story being written, a story being produced, and a story in post-production. Those are the most important of your multiple targets - and part of your job is to free your mental bandwidth to make sure they are right from jump street, and that you muster the necessary fortitude and stamina to work with the denizens of the writers room - annoying though they may be.

This is why conveying your vision clearly, and delegating the conveyance of that vision to others is so important.

Now, if you do all that, and you still can't simultaneously work on the story in development, the two stories on the page, the story on the set, and the story in post-production without becoming confused and cranky... you might want to consider becoming a novelist.

THE EIGHTH LAW OF SHOWRUNNING
RESIST THE SIREN CALL OF THE "SEXY GLAMOROUS JOBS" - ESPECIALLY POST-PRODUCTION
SERIOUSLY.
STAY AWAY FROM POST-PRODUCTION FOR AS LONG AS HUMANLY POSSIBLE

We are in the business of entertaining people. It then stands to reason that many facets of the process of entertaining people are entertaining in and of themselves... especially when the alternative to these amusements is to skulk into a room full of lousy, ungrateful writers sitting around waiting for you to tell them how to tell your story.

And what's fun about that? The writers are shouty, and judgy, and kinda - what's the best way of saying this? - possessing of their own individual identities and preoccupations that have nothing to do with you. They don't appreciate your unique genius like they should, the room stinks of take-out food and desperation, and the stories don't even exist yet!

In that room, you have to figure out everything from scratch, and make sure that one scene causes the next, and that the design of the entire season arc makes logical sense, and that the dozens of characters in the series are having complicated emotions.

It's <u>hard</u>!

You know where's fun? The place where they make the costumes. Oh - it's awesome over there. They have drawings of pretty girls on the walls, the costumers are frequently young and attractive - and have a great sense of style and design - and, every once in a while, beautiful actors come in and put on a fashion show for you!

The same applies for the production design and prop

fabrication offices - festooned as they are with blueprints, concept art, fabric samples, and awesome gizmos in various stages of construction. And if you like that, wait 'til you hit the VFX office, where the boffins will regale you with endless, and gallantly woven, tales of pre-vis and fluid dynamics simulations!

Oh, and then there's casting. That's where you can hear actors come in and say your lines in every manner possible... imagine that: pretty people come in and say your beautiful words back to you, and you get to JUDGE them with impunity!

These are what I call "the sexy, glamorous jobs."

You can convince yourself that your direct supervision of these tasks is of the essence... especially if you are stuck on a difficult story knot and the other writers keep telling you the direction you want to go isn't going to untangle it.

There's another pernicious aspect to becoming too enamored of the sexy glamorous jobs: the longer you spend with your other departments - exploring all the options, deferring your decisions, being generally unclear about your aesthetic goals, and being dazed by all the pretty pictures people are showing you - the more you rob from them the time they need to actually do their job: the designing and construction of things that will look great before the camera and not just sound great in your conversation...

And, by and large, most of them will be too nice to tell you to go away and let them work.

That's one of the reasons it's so pleasant for the showrunner to go to a lot of these meetings outside the writers room. Unlike the writers - whose role as creative partners and your closest advisors gives them some leave to call you out on your shit - most of the other departments cannot.

Remember, they know damn well you can fire anyone who displeases you - and they are petrified that you will throw a hand grenade into the work they have already completed - so they will indulge your conversational needs and make you feel like you're a wit on par with Oscar Wilde and the Second Coming of Joss Whedon. That's part of the siren song of the sexy glamorous jobs.

So don't be a Time Bandit (or a "Time Vampire," both terms used by staffers I have known to describe malingering showrunners seeking refuge from the the writers room). Tell people what you want concisely and efficiently... and then <u>leave</u>...

Or better yet, tell one of your writer/producers what you want, let them have the discussion with the different department heads first, and then make course corrections later when there's an adequate level of proof of concept.

All of this brings me to post-production.

There was a time when post-production was the most ignored and insular department in TV production. The mechanics by which episodes were edited and finished were analog, artisanal, and very painstaking and time-consuming in a way wholly incompatible with the fast pace of television production: literally requiring the splicing of bits of film with sticky tape by hobbits working in moist, mossy caves.

Back then, an episode would have to be edited, then screened in a theater for the showrunner and producers, who would give their notes either verbally or via memos, and then the film would be sent back to the hobbits, who would meticulously (no, seriously, they had to wear gloves) pull the strips of film apart from the sticky tape, re-cut the film by hand to make the necessary adjustments, splice the entire kit and kaboodle back together with more sticky tape, and then screen it again for everyone's approval.

In the late twentieth century - thanks to advances in computer software and memory, and the development of the non-linear/non-destructive editing workflow - post-production changed from a fairly recondite process to becoming the single most seductive time suck for showrunners seeking refuge from their actual job.

As anyone who has ever used iMovie can tell you, picture editing is now like having a word processor for a movie - a movie that you wrote (or rewrote and thus rescued from mediocrity). Honestly, there's a reason I refer to it as a siren's call - if Narcissus were a showrunner, the editing room would be his reflecting pool.

A showrunner can now go into the editing suite (usually a warmly lit, air-conditioned room with a large leather couch put there to appease the local Hutts, and massive high-definition screens with a pipeline to the editing system) and watch an episode, a sequence, a scene - even a single sequence of shots - over and over again, and demand any change that enters his/her mind... and, thanks to the miracle of computerized cut-and-paste and endless levels of "undo" and "redo", see it all in real time, and continue to demand changes until every combination of every frame that was shot has been considered. (Not to mention that with all that raw computing power, you can spend days choosing just the right temp soundtrack, and putting in makeshift VFX and titles and transitions - and basically creating something amazingly polished that almost looks like a real TV show...)

It's like getting ACTUAL work done.

Only it's not.

Really. It isn't. It only looks that way.

Though a humongous boon to the art and craft of television, the rise of non-linear/non-destructive post-production has also created an entire class of parasitic troglodytes (usually non-writing producers desperate to justify their meddling ways) who rally under the despicable war cry of "I'm GREAT in post!"

You wanna know what the words "I'm GREAT in post" in the mouth of most producers are really dog whistle code for? "I will gladly sit on that leather couch for an eternity and hound your helpless editor into an assisted suicide."

I mean it. Someone invented the AVID and the next thing you know, everyone and their mother is Pablo fuckin' Ferro.

It stinks.

That's not to mean that there aren't producers - writing and non-writing - who are, in fact, GREAT in post. There are, and their contribution is invaluable. They are also a small, and gifted, and rare species. Kind of like unicorns and shootable first drafts.

If you are a showrunner and you're wondering whether or not you're great in post, then you probably aren't.

If you are a showrunner and you find a non-writing producer who is demonstrably great in post, then hire them, pay them well, and use them to keep you out of the editing bay for as long as possible.

Look. I get it. Eventually, all showrunners will have to spend some time sitting on that leather couch frame-fucking the work. We're messianic visionaries with an idiosyncratic "creative process," and it's inevitable.

The trick to maintaining a healthy balance between the

editing room and the writers room is to not fool yourself into thinking that post-production is where the show truly is - and to recognize that, more often than not, post is where the fearful go to hide from their writers.

I have encountered many truly egregious offenders in this respect - more than one whose work I guarantee you respect and admire - whose ratio of hours spent in editing versus time spent in the writers room that was easily ten to one. All of them insisted that they had to spend all that time in editing because that's how their "creative process" worked. When pressed, each and every one of them assured me that they needed the time in editing to "find the show."

And every time I politely bit my tongue when what I should have done was suggest that maybe they were looking for the show in the wrong place. If you need to find the show in post, chances are you lost it in the writers room. It's a simple calculus: showrunners who put in the time in the writers room seldom have to bunker in editing trying to reverse-engineer the story that was actually filmed into the story in their minds.

The result of these showrunners' contempt for the writers room - and their penchant for torturing editors - causes a vicious cycle. Having only enough patience to sign off on the broadest strokes of a story, these showrunners are invariably "surprised" by the material they receive at either script or outline. Then they insist on re-breaking the story - often in awkward one-to-one sessions that do little else than reaffirm the showrunners' dislike for the process. Eventually, this all results in the showrunner completely rewriting the script very late in the process to the detriment of everyone.

Such showrunners eventually blame everyone but themselves for the "poor quality" of the film they receive from the set, and furiously retreat to post-production to "find" the episode. Rinse and repeat.

This sort of "arsonist/firefighter/last minute savior" stupidity is endemic in the ranks of showrunners... and the ease with which digital, non-linear, non-destructive editing has made it possible for the show to be rewritten in post-production shoulders a great deal of the blame.

So how do you mitigate the siren call? By keeping your eye on the story, and by delegating to those who know the story best the task of making sure that the cut has been maximized toward the telling of the story before you step into the editing room (unsurprisingly, most director's cuts - which are always the first version of the story shown to the writer/producers per union rules - prioritize the director's visual flair over more prosaic concerns like pacing and clarity of narrative).

So let's say you're the showrunner and the director's cut has just been finished. Instead of going into the editing room to watch it from the leather couch - and start frame fucking before the theme music kicks up - watch it on a DVD in your office with the editor and the episode writer. Have a thorough discussion with them as to whether the scenes are telling the story (concerns of style and flair can wait until the story is solid) while an assistant takes notes, and then send the editor off to perform the notes.

When the editor is ready with the next iteration of the episode, do NOT look at it. Send the writer of the episode in to look at the next cut and let him or her decide whether the notes were addressed and give the next round of feedback: again, focussing on whether or not the film is telling the story.

Only after you've allowed these steps to take place - maybe more than once - should you get on the leather couch and make it sing. When you begin to work this way, you may feel like you're abandoning a child during a crucial developmental stage, but I promise you - what you are doing is giving the children being conceived a fighting chance at life.

Now, just because I am an advocate of delegating to your staff doesn't mean I am blind to the truth that even a person of your impeccable good taste and judgment could, potentially make a bad staffing decision here and there. Purely accidentally, of course.

It is a sad truth that not all of your hires may be up to the tasks you assign for them, but before you break out the pink slips, you may want to consider...

THE NINTH LAW OF SHOWRUNNING
EXPECT YOUR STAFF TO PERFORM AT VARYING LEVELS OF COMPETENCE

As I mentioned previously, you are not just running a corporation, but also a spoke of the apprentice-to-master wheel which many of your writers will ride all the way to becoming senior-level writer/producers and showrunners themselves. You may neither want - nor be qualified, or fitted by temperament - to be a teacher and a mentor, but, as that poignant, and now-classic, song goes, "Whoomp, there it is."

Among the many keys to being a successful mentor is the understanding that - when you have a room full of writers of different ranks and levels of ability - they will all perform on the page, and in the writers room, differently.

The executive producer-level writer with twenty-five

years of experience - the person who ran his or her own show last year and is now on your staff as your Number Two - should be reliably expected to turn in drafts in which the scene structures will be solid, the characters will speak with a voice close to what you have established (provided you have been following the Second Law with some measure of diligence), and the dialogue will sparkle with not only style and brio, but also reflect in every movement the emotional state of the characters as you have designed it for not just the one episode, but also the sweep of the series. You may not ultimately like this writer's execution of the material - that part is subjective - but you should have no doubt upon reading their work that you are in the hands of a pro.

This is what your senior-level writer/producer has been doing for twenty-five years: learning how to solve story problems in script, mastering the craft of creating scenes that have a discrete beginning, middle, and end - perhaps with a memorable button/punch-line - figuring out how to weave the prosaic concerns of plot and theme into dialogue that conceals the storytelling machinery beneath, and gaining mastery over all of the different patterns by which scenes ebb and flow into one another... all in the service of giving you - the showrunner - a reading experience that will not only sound to you like your own voice, but like your own voice peppered with the mastery of an accomplished craftsman so skilled in the ways of hiding his or her own genius that you mistake it for your own.

The assistant who got to share a story credit last season, and whom you promoted to staff writer a week ago as a reward for their loyalty, hard work, and support - and because you read a spec script of theirs that you don't really know how long they took to write (or how much input they had from others in its creation) - cannot be expected to deliver on that level. It's on you to not only budget your time and energy accordingly to both give them thoughtful notes and rewrite their material, but also to muster the *largesse* to judge their work more leniently: to recognize where that beginning writer has performed at - or above and beyond - their level of skill.

To most showrunners, this seems exceptionally unfair... and it is, to be honest, something of a damned nuisance. After all, staff writers have the freedom to share their opinion and ideas in the colloquium of the writers room - and, frankly, many denizens of the lower levels avail themselves of that right way too freely when what they should be doing is shutting the fuck up and learning. Hell, just yesterday one of the staff writers had the audacity to suggest that one of your ideas wasn't all that good - and they didn't even have the good taste to pitch something with which to replace it! So why is it on you to grade them on a curve?

Because it's on you to help them achieve the level of mastery where their scripts look and read like those of the twenty-five-year veteran. That's why. Just like it's also on you to make them responsible citizens of the writers room, and suggest to them when it's OK to criticize and when to hold back.

Similarly, the process by which you give notes to your writers isn't some cargo cult where you park a script to spin its palm-frond-and-coconut turboprops until you have the time to save it with your rewriting genius. The better and more well-considered your feedback and tutelage, the better the scripts your writers will produce. And it isn't some glacial process: give your staff the most accurate and specific information about what you want, and the most constructive feedback as to the how and why (and yes, describing to them WHAT to write counts - don't think they will resent your telling them exactly what you want the scene to look/sound like), and you will see marked improvement from script to script.

Funny how simple that sounds, and yet, many showrunners just can't wrap their heads around that concept. Sometimes it's just more expedient and less exhausting to give a younger writer a bunch of busywork until you find the time to fix it yourself.

It's also wrong, and a disservice to your trade.

But do it you must... and, hey, at the end of the season, or the conclusion of the writers' contracts - you can always fire those writers who don't "get it"...

But you know what you DON'T get to do? (Well, you can do it all you want, actually - most showrunners do - but you can't call yourself "a human being" in my book if you do.) You don't get to read the staff writer's first draft - oftentimes the first thing this person has written under the time and content restrictions of a writing staff - and say "wow, they just don't 'get it' and I'm going to fire them."

You hired them. You teach them.

More work, Sparky, I know. But... as the now-classic song taught us all: "It's hard out here for a pimp."

The flip side of the atrocities described above is the following ubiquitous and nasty little bit of stupidity - usually perpetrated by showrunners who wrongheadedly fancy themselves "men of the people" - the privileging of notes and feedback from "trusted" outsiders over that of experienced professionals.

One showrunner for whom I worked a few years back insisted that he could not finalize a pilot script until he got notes from the line cook at his childhood hometown diner... it was his way of making sure he stayed "real."

While this was the most extreme version of this delusion that I have encountered, it's not that far on the end of the spectrum from the many, many showrunners who believed that bullshit some other successful showrunner once said in a WGA magazine interview about "the best idea should win, I don't care WHERE it comes from," and shows this fealty to their trade unionist roots by continually calling in the twenty-five-year-old who runs the phones in the reception area to tell the twenty-five-year veteran "that idea you had the other day about how to make this script better."

Though my harsh response to this scenario - which I have encountered to a vomitous extreme over the length of my career (hell, I was once the twenty-five-year-old in question, I thought it was awesome to be consulted, and later paid for the favor in blood) - may, on the surface, seem like the parochial upholding of hierarchical entitlement by a threatened old-timer, here's why it's a horrible thing to do...

A. By the time a pitch/outline/script comes to you, the writers room has undoubtedly discussed it to every possible endgame: <u>that's their job</u>. The assistant's idea may sound great on the face of it, but you were probably in post-production when it came up in the room and was considered. More likely than not, it was already tossed around, taken for a test drive, kicked on the tires, and judged wanting for reasons that you have not yet had the time to examine.

B. You have also - and whether you think this is the more senior writer being too sensitive, you did it anyway - told the person whom you should be trusting with the stewardship of your vision that you, frankly, don't really trust them all that much with the stewardship of your vision. It's a tone-deaf, disempowering, rookie mistake that - more often than not - indicates a pattern of disrespect and disempowerment.

C. You have sent the message that it's OK for a young and inexperienced person to speak out against a superior. That's not a sin necessarily, but applied capriciously and frequently, it does breed in the writers room a weird entitlement in which junior members of the staff wind up holding back the process because they now believe they have authority above their position. You wonder why the room feels so spiky, and is so full of Napoleonic junior writers who have so high an esteem for their own criticism of your ideas? Wonder, instead, whether you are encouraging this behavior.

D. You have put the younger member of the hierarchy in the awkward position of being shut down in front of you - the supreme leader - by another one of his/her mentors. It's a scenario in which everyone loses face and feels like shit except for you. You get to go on with your life thinking you're a "man of the people" because everyone is too afraid to tell you otherwise... but the truth is, the younger member of the staff hates you for making them pitch to someone who now wants to punch you in the face by proxy by punching them in the face... and the cycle continues.

E. You are perpetuating the fiction that you are a "nice person" and a "good boss" when what you are in fact doing is privileging the counsel of people whose power differential with yours is so steep that they will never actually question your decisions in a productive way. You think you are fomenting the genius of the

precocious and prodigious, but what you are in fact
doing is creating a cult of personality in the form of
skewed, dysfunctional mentor/mentee relationships
that will damage the conduct and career of your
charges down the line.

Now let's say that the young man or woman who answers
the phones in the front office comes to you with an idea
that you do find undeniable and beguiling. How do you
present it to your staff without triggering the apocalypse of
awkwardness described above?

You give the note yourself without the youngling in
the room - if it succeeds the tests, you then graciously give
credit to the youngling, also preferably without them in
the room, and then later let them know that their idea is
being used and that everyone knows where it came from.
If the idea is proven to have already been talked about and
discarded - and you realize you yourself are behind the
mainstream of the creative process in your own room by
pitching it - you take it on the chin, shrug it off as a brain
fart and move on. Showrunners never lose face when they
admit to a brain fart - in fact, it makes them kind of adorbs.

Conversely, if you are the youngest/least experienced/
lowest-ranked writer on a staff and have an objection to
the work of a more senior writer (and I am only giving this
advice here because it behooves showrunners to teach this
kind of behavior), and have an idea as to how you might
fix it (if you don't, you are - in the words of the Dowager
Countess - about as useful as a glass hammer), then run
your criticism/idea by the next person from you in the
hierarchy... and maybe then go with that person to the next
person up. You build consensus, ensure that the ground
under your feet is solid, and then throw the hand grenade.

These last two points do bring up one, frequently very difficult managerial conundrum - what do you do when your writers room truly includes a bad apple? Does that fall under the rubric of "expecting writers to behave at different levels of competence?"

Actually, it absolutely does - but that doesn't mean you have to tolerate it, and there are a lot of very useful strategies to mitigate the damage done by negative actors in your staff.

Let's begin by identifying the three most common kinds of bad apples that show up in writers' staffs and rooms:

1. The "Doctor No" - A writer who responds to most ideas that are not theirs with "that sucks" and then proceeds to let everyone know - usually in breathtakingly explicit detail - how and why the idea sucks... usually without providing any concrete advice about how to fix the problem. Especially cancerous Doctor Noes will sometimes make a practice of coming back days - or even weeks - after the idea has been accepted and put to work in the DNA of the story and bringing things to a grinding halt by explaining why it sucks, of course, never offering any helpful hints as to how to actually... you know... fix the problem.

2. The "Hostage Taker" - Sometimes, Doctor Noes take such pleasure oraculating about their objections that they cross the line into Hostage Taker. I once had the misfortune of running a room in which the local Doctor No, upon making his objections clear, would - if they were not immediately, and diligently addressed by the rest of the staff as a hot rush life-or-death crisis - put on a hundred yard pout, whip out a cellphone, and conspicuously play Doodle Jump while emitting

as many Huffs and Snorts as necessary to ensure that no one could move forward without acknowledging his displeasure. Another brand of hostage-taking, not related to Doctor No-ism, comes from the writer who mistakes the safe and open environment of the ideal room - to which its participants should be able to bring their personal business, within the understood parameters of it being germane and additive to the story - for their own psychotherapy session/PhD thesis defense. For these hostage takers, time is a Philip Glassian concept, and the sound of their own voice is Black Tar Heroin.

3. The Politician/Manipulator/Insulter - This, of course, refers to those people who, through either tone deafness, a desire to be heard and provoke at any cost the laughter and delight that daddy never found in their wit, or just plain old-fashioned sociopathic malice, use information divulged in the open forum of the writers room to either publicly or privately hurt, undermine, or make a punchline out of the other writers. This disease can be especially pernicious, because the room runs on a certain amount of trust and sensitivity, and repairing that trust is an exponential investment of time from the speed with which it can be broken. Sometimes, this brand of Bad Apple-ism cannot be corrected: some assholes just love the feeling of power that comes from Making Others Feel Like Shit.

The strategies you need to correct these problems are simple and straightforward. Oftentimes the people doing these things do not realize that they are doing them - showrunning is so full of incompetent senior management that many people will go through entire careers without realizing that they are behaving badly.

Correcting bad behavior is one of your jobs, even if most showrunners don't do it because it requires... gulp... confrontation. Here are the five simplest ways of clearing your barrels of the Bad Apples...

1. Throw the problem back at Doctor No - This one is simple, easy, and works 95% of the time. Doctor No tells you that they disapprove of something, you tell them "You break it, you bought it." Your perception of a problem is worse than useless if you do not have a fix. If you can pitch an objection, but not a solution, you have not earned the right to speak. As showrunner, you get to express that to your writers, first in the most polite way possible, and then in escalating levels of exasperation until it sticks. In rooms I have run, I simply make a declaration of this early and often - you don't get to criticize if you don't show up in overalls with a toolbox. More importantly, expressing this is an important part of your job as a teacher: most writers' critical faculty develops earlier than the more craft-focused, patience-requiring, spade-and-trowel discipline of story generation and repair. If you don't correct this behavior early and often, you are causing yourself and other showrunners a lot more trouble down the line.

2. Confront the problem early, head on, and earnestly - You may think that you have to come up with an artful way of bringing up a difficult interpersonal issue to a staff member. Guess what? You don't. Leave the florid writing and brilliant scene structures for the page. If someone is chronically hijacking the room, tell them firmly, but politely (and preferably privately), that

"You have a tendency to overshare, it's not always useful, and it undermines the times when what you have to say helps move the story forward," or "You need to watch the jokes about people's personal lives, they come across as hurtful," or (and this was once said to me - and to this day, I thank the bearer of this statement) "Your graphic descriptions of your self-loathing and body image issues are making the other writers uncomfortable, you may want to take your hand off the throttle." Life is not a script, and you don't have to be excessively artful - or artfully impolite and cruel - to tell people what you need from them. If they push back, don't engage or become defensive, hear them out, and let them know that they have been heard but that - their defense notwithstanding - you have identified a problem and want it worked on. This is often a crucial aspect of problem-solving: <u>a lot of people just want to know that they are on the record, even if it doesn't change the outcome</u>. Remember, you're not paid to be anyone's best friend, and you're not a Man of the People: you're the boss.

3. Discuss the problem with your closest subordinate, have them deal with it in one of the ways described above, and save your intervention as a court of final appeal - The reason a twenty-five-year veteran is being well-paid to be your right hand is because they bring the experience and weight to deal with problems like this. Use them: decide which of you is to be the good cop, which of you is to be the bad cop, let them deal with the problem, have their back, and if the recalcitrant writer insists on not changing, use the power of your office to reinforce the message at a later time. If, in spite of all this, the pushback becomes so

strident that you soon realize this person will not be taught, then there's always the nuclear options:

4. Exile - The Doctor No I described previously eventually proved so unwilling to step back on the endless, process-killing objections about the quality of the show - and the capacity of the writing staff to address them - that it was eventually necessary to figure out a better use for his talent. This writer was given scene writing assignments on multiple scripts by the showrunner - who genuinely valued his work on the page - and kept out of the writers room altogether. Over the course of several shows, I have often seen incorrigibly narcissistic Hostage Takers sent to perform producorial services on the set - where a willingness to argue, clarify, and pontificate is often a boon instead of a liability. So much of what happens on the set is about clarifying - especially for the actors - the context of the work at hand, so these hostage-takers often blossom there. This is not an optimal solution: writers are paid to write and contribute ideas, but sometimes, writers are so incompatible with the collaborative process that you may find yourself cornered into having to find an alternate use for their talents, at least until you can let them go, and they can be hired on another show that might have a culture more suited to their personal style.

5. Fire their time-sucking ass - Sometimes, there's just no two ways about it. Firing people sucks. I've done it and it's nowhere as satisfying as it looks on *The Apprentice*. It's stressful and emotionally draining. The merciful way (once you have dotted all your i's and crossed all your t's with the studio's HR) is to rip off the Band-Aid and be done with it, then everyone can move on.

I know, Sparky, it's all so complicated. Like court machinations in the Ming Dynasty. Can't we all just be comrades and equals? One person, one vote?

No. We can't.

We all want to pretend there are geniuses and prodigies in all of the inexperienced people we hire - mostly because it bolsters the idea that we ourselves came from the ranks of the genial and prodigious. The truth is, however, that you gain mastery over the form and function of television in the same way that chess players master their game: by studying old games, internalizing the patterns, and practicing, practicing, practicing. Lay-people mistake both chess and writing as explosions of genius-level creativity - but where does the black powder for that explosion come from?

It comes from pattern recognition. That's why the twenty-five-year veteran is usually so good at the job of breaking story, even if the younger writers demonstrate a greater flair for dialogue, or can render the rhythms of the current popular culture with greater fidelity. Veterans don't have to reinvent the wheel every time out. The veteran looks at the notecards on the board and recognizes the ten different ways the game can go from that point to a win, or a draw, or a defeat.

There are only so many variations in chess and in story telling - the reason you rely on the experience of the veteran is that they don't have to play every variation in order to predict how to reach the outcome you want. The art of writing is in how you disguise the mechanics of this assembly, just as the art of chess comes from fooling your opponent into not seeing your endgame thirty moves ahead.

You may be tempted by the idea of a cabinet of equals,

marching in lockstep and doing what's best for the creative process - but your job is to lead and to teach, not to be loved. You earn love by recognizing that everyone's gifts are different and giving your employees an environment in which is it safe to try, and both succeed and fail.

Every member of a writing staff is, in some way, on the hook for the education of the next person below them; recognizing that everyone is working at a different level is your first step toward building camaraderie. All that pretending that all animals are equal ever gets to is the embarrassing revelation that some are more equal than others, and to you looking like an asshole.

Hierarchy is not a dirty word. Hierarchy is not the sign of a hidebound mind that resists change and innovation. Hierarchy is not proof that you're a square and sell-out. Properly enacted, and thoughtfully maintained, hierarchy is the flak jacket that allows each member of your staff to reach their highest potential without being shredded by gunfire.

THE TENTH LAW OF SHOWRUNNING
DELIVER GOOD AND BAD NEWS EARLY AND OFTEN

Though I have beat to the ground the analogy of television show as startup corporation, the time has come for me to admit that - being as it may - a television show is also something of a wandering circus, with tents, and instruments, and artisans, and sideshows... and all the dramas that come along when you force a hundred or more people into close communion under the pressure cooker that is intense work performed under great stress for a defined period of time.

Invariably, drama comes from secrets. In my

experience, secrets are poison - especially when you are exposed as their bearer. Sunlight is the best disinfectant.

The Tenth Law of showrunning is a close dependent of the Second: as the sun source of the show's vision and the one best qualified to say What It Is and What It Is Not, make the ripping of Band-Aids your business, rumor control your secondary vocation, and complete transparency your ultimate goal...

And save the drama for the screen.

The reasons for this are of the essence of the First and Second Laws. You want and need to be the source of all that is true about your show - even if that truth is unpleasant. The worst position for a leader is as the bearer of bad news everyone already knows.

Any information that aids the speed and efficiency of creation - even if it hurts feelings - is worth exposing early, tactfully, and often... and if that information exposes you as the cause of a blunder, you are better off putting your pride aside and owning up than expecting everyone who works for you become the unwilling accomplices in - and hostages of - the protection of your own delicate sensibilities.

Whenever a rumor, a lie, or a truth that you have not sanctioned takes on a life of its own, it undermines your own ability to set the tone, define the parameters, and describe a path to success.

One of the more famous Hollywood memoirs is titled *Which Lie Did I Tell?* (Although my personal favorite title of a Hollywood memoir is *What Just Happened?*)

Anyway, the title connotes a certain lack of remorse; the idea that part of the swingin' fun of makin' movies is a certain commitment to juggling deceptions until the final product is done and the chips fall where they may. The problem is that, where movies are, in contrast, fly-by-night operations, success in television means a long haul in close quarters: most lies, and their tellers, lack the stamina to survive for long.

To me, transparency is not just a moral imperative to the life of a showrunner; it's a necessary lifeline. If you need to devote one iota of your energy to deception tracking and maintenance, that's an iota that's not going to the work you need to accomplish in the writers room. Hell, that energy would be better spent doing any one of the sexy glamorous jobs.

Transparency streamlines your life. Being transparent before anyone can be transparent for you means you control the narrative. Giving bad news before they crash land means no one can claim surprise at a bad break. The best thing a showrunner can say in the face of a difficult situation - especially to networks and studios, whose institutional memory is that of a goldfish and whose capacity to accept the blame for anything is nil - is "You can't say I didn't tell you this was coming."

Well, that, and "Here's the solution, you don't have to worry. I got this."

When everyone knows the truth, no one can be surprised by its arrival. When it comes from you, no one can say that you lost control. And we all know that if there's something that showrunners love, it's control... sweet, sweet control.

Well, control and one other thing... the last thing you have to sacrifice if you actually want to be good at this job. Are you ready, Sparky? This one's gonna hurt in the short term, but in the long term, it's the one that's going to make you look most like a prince...

THE ELEVENTH LAW OF SHOWRUNNING
SHARE CREDIT FOR SUCCESS TO A FAULT

The Eleventh and final Law of showrunning is the tail of the snake in the mouth of the First...

Never miss an opportunity to point out how another person's work has made you look good. It's your name on the show and it's all about you anyway, so you lose nothing by sharing credit.

I know that it sounds counter-intuitive. I know you feel embattled, and suspect that everyone is out to get you - even your own writers, whom you secretly believe write poorly on purpose just to spite, frazzle, and drive you to an early grave - and that everyone wants you to fail and prove your daddy right... so you must fight to be recognized as the creative genius behind every success.

I get it... but I have been through to the other side and have come back to tell you - and I know this one's a difficult one to swallow - you don't.

And you know why? That recognition comes to you weekly in the form of the largest paycheck on the payroll, the biggest office in the suite, the parking spot closest to the front door, and the brand new Tesla in that spot, and the Executive Producer credit in the main titles of every episode of the show - along with your production company card after the end titles.

Everyone knows who and what you are. Everyone is hanging on your words. You have no need to hoard what belongs to others in the name of gaining recognition for your struggles, however arduous and hard-fought they may seem.

In my twenty years, I have, regrettably, but not at all surprisingly, witnessed literally dozens, if not hundreds, of interactions between showrunners and network or studio executives in which the showrunner has - either purposefully or, even worse, casually and without concern or understanding of the ramifications - said something like: "If the last draft [NAME OF WRITER] handed to me is any indication, you won't be seeing that script for a while" or "The truth is, I had to rewrite every page [NAME OF WRITER] ever gave me" or the hardy perennial "I have to rewrite ALL the scripts from page one" or "[NAME OF WRITER] really boned me with that draft," or the jolly old chestnut: "If only I could find a staff of writers that could just do my show."

For this type of showrunner, even praise comes from the left hand with a price in flesh and blood. I'm reminded of the fucking douchebag (yes, another person whose work I guarantee you respect and admire) who once said to me - at a cocktail party and within earshot of several members of his writing staff - "Well, I got the first round of scripts and the good news is at least I don't have to fire anyone... yet" (cue "charming" devilish grin).

Two things happen when you make comments like this in any context other than the actual moment at the actual end of the actual season when you actually have to take stock and make the actual decision to actually fire a staff member...

One: Your venting of your temporary frustration with a bad draft or an incompatible hiring choice to the Powers That Be at the studio and network colors their perception of that writer FAR longer than you can possibly know. That's right, Sparky, you may have just shanked someone's career to make yourself feel better.

Two: You come across as a whiny fucking anhedonic little shit who has no concept of how good they have it.

You know all those network executives who listen to your troubles and trials, and sound - on the phone, and over countless sushi lunches - like they feel your pain?

They don't.

The network and studio are more invested in the success and longevity of the show than they are in the success and longevity of you. It's a distinction with a subtle, but massive difference.

Need an example? *The West Wing* outlasted Aaron Sorkin for three seasons. An extreme example, to be sure, but the studio made damned sure the show made it to syndication, turned a profit, and kept its place in all those "top twenty/thirty/forty/fifty series of all time" lists with or without him. Though the show was definitely seen as lacking the spark that made Sorkin's seasons a cultural event, John Wells's stewardship of the studio's precious resource produced a very respectable and stable series whose merits remained defendable to the very last day.

Also - and it gives me no pleasure to report this, Sparky - studio and network are certainly not invested in furthering your self-concept as a put-upon genius suffering a confederacy of dunces hellbent on holding back your brave attempts at self-expression. It sounds mean and mercenary, but it's called "show business," not "show friends" - and when they hear you throwing other writers under the bus, their words to you may be sympathetic, but what they are thinking isn't "Oh, poor, sweet, hard-working Sparky," but rather, "Sparky seems to have a very hard time making good hiring decisions and his inability to put together a functioning staff may become a liability, let's file that away for his next contract negotiation."

So there you go: two good reasons not to be the kind of showrunner who doesn't liberally share credit for success with his or her staff. One, it makes you sound like a fucking douchebag. Two, it makes you sound like an INCOMPETENT fucking douchebag.

The wonderful thing about credit is that it's not a finite resource. Now, I know that, somewhere along the line, someone made you believe that the credit dinosaurs were crushed under the Earth's crust a billion years ago, and it's all running out, and you have to hoard the stuff like you're fuckin' Smeagol.

Maybe it was your daddy who told you this instead of letting you know that he loved you, and so you feel like you must now follow his lead just in case it really is running out. But it's just not true. And, in all honesty, now that we are really getting to know one another, I'm really starting to think that your daddy is just not a good source for truth.

The truth is this: the more credit you give, the more credit you get - for being a genius and hiring a great staff, for being a good boss and a nice person (finally!) who can acknowledge the contributions of others, for fostering a positive work environment, and - most crucially - for being the kind of showrunner who <u>protects their writers from the kinds of short term judgments that you have the liberty to rethink in the long term</u>.

And yet there will be times when the studio or network will ask for a draft that you are not prepared to hand over because you need to do a lot of work on it because the writers didn't nail it. You know what you say?

You say: "There's still work to be done." That's it. You won't sound incompetent. You won't sound like a fucking douchebag. If there is pushback from the studio or network, take the responsibility yourself: own it and revel in the truth that you are SO big, and powerful, and OZ-like, that a blow that would cripple the career of someone of lesser rank is but a ding on your door.

And it's one of those plastic minivan doors that bounces back after the shopping cart hits it, by the way... the ding vanishes - as if by magic - the moment you turn in the script and it's great.

The reason this is the final Law of Showrunning is not just that it feeds right back into the First Law, but also that it is the biggest test of character before you as someone who has just been handed something close to absolute power in the business.

How you deal with praise - and success, and all the concomitant slings and arrows thrown at you for your position - and whether you recognize that you have within you the strength to be that aforementioned flak jacket to your staff, is as true a test of your self-esteem and worth as a person as anything you will ever face.

As a senior manager you have the ability to either make your show and bring up with you an entire class of people who will credit you for their learning and empowerment... or to make your show with a huge amount of staff turnover, a reputation for being difficult, and a great deal of overwork heaped upon you by your own inability to earn your staff's loyalty.

Again, because I feel very strongly about this, I am going to go ahead and hit below the belt once more... forgive me, Sparky, but here it goes...

You don't earn daddy's love by hoarding all the good stuff and claiming it as your entitlement. You defeat daddy - and shame him into respect and admiration - by raising an entire generation of daughters and sons who don't perpetuate his legacy of abuse and abandonment. You make daddy look at you and see something he never made, and, in that way, you make him finally understand his own loss.

And then you forgive him.

CONCLUSION AND FINAL INSULT

Now we come to the part where you say something like... "But what about the undeniable truth that I can only do my best work in the late night/early morning while the prettiest assistant in the bullpen sits on the couch listening to me talk out my ideas?" (I am sorry to report that I've been told firsthand that this has been standard practice on a number of shows whose creators you respect and admire)...

Or "But if I can't see every possible version of every possible scene in the edit bay, I will never be able to live with myself knowing that the final product could have been something better!" (this is a paraphrase of an actual quote spoken to me)...

Or "The writers room is all fine and dandy, but the only time I can really relax is when the writers come to my house on the weekends, where I can smoke and drink without all those pesky workplace safety regulations and really let the creative juices flow away from the hustle-and-bustle and distractions," (I've had to do this one once or twice in my career)...

Or "How can I possibly reset my creative energies unless EVERYONE participates in the mandatory all-office 10PM pinball elimination tournament?" (You hear this story around town a lot, I'm not sure who the culprit is... and sometimes it's foosball instead of pinball. In some versions of the story, the senior members of the staff eventually stage an intervention and beg that the tournament be suspended so the writers and support staff can go home to their families an hour earlier... and after much consideration, the showrunner comes back with "fuckit - no - this is my process!")...

Or maybe you're thinking "All those <u>other</u> shows may have writing styles that can be taught, but mine is so unique and different that only I can render it in a way that satisfies my inner metronome," (Not a direct quote, but expressed by multiple showrunners - oftentimes as a badge of pride)...

Or "All this talk of management, and strategy, and humility is fine and dandy for ordinary hacks who are willing to settle for less, but I'm a demanding perfectionist!" (I'd be lying to you if I told you I ever heard anyone put it that bluntly, but I promise, it's not an uncommon sentiment)...

Or just plain "What about my 'creative process'?"

Well, shit, Sparky... I thought we could be friends...

Remember that point I made early on about how much ego it takes to be a TV writer? Well, you clearly have bags of that, and it's obviously deceived you into believing that you might just be the lone exception to everything I just said.

And now - since the last eighteen-thousand words have obviously failed to convince you - I'm gonna have to Call Down The Thunder:

Shut the fuck up about your creative process.

That's what about your creative process.

Your "creative process" is what you did in the dark with your Speed Racer jammies around your ankles while mommy and daddy slept in the next room. Your "creative process" is the fiction you peddle to magazines when you're successful. Your "creative process" is the way you punish yourself and others for the unpardonable sin of being good at a job daddy didn't approve of but secretly wanted for himself.

Between just the two of us here in our grown-up dungarees, we both know damn well that there isn't a single writer who works for money who - when the time comes - can't just <u>sit the fuck down and bang it the fuck out</u>.

Now, guess what? Every single day of your life while your show is on the air is that time.

The price you pay to play on the world stage and sermonize to an audience of millions is that you have to make concessions between the tempestuous *artiste* you idealized for yourself when you thought working in TV was the equivalent of being put on the train to Hogwarts and the reality that you are now a grown-ass adult professional who earns more for producing a single episode of television than most people do in a year.

The price of admission to the Majors is that you now have people who depend on you: not just for their living, but also their creative, emotional - and, occasionally, physical - well-being...

And, oh yes, you also have an audience that's waiting to be entertained.

Your creativity is going to be fine - it was always fine - and it will always be fine. Your creativity is a renewable resource - just like praise, and credit, and the simple, and difficult truth that your daddy's neglect wasn't really your fault.

No, really. It was probably the result of his own abuse at the hands of your grandfather and had nothing to do with you as a person.

Your creativity is fed by everything around you -

especially the great people you hired to facilitate this difficult undertaking. Your creativity is not some finite thing that must be hoarded and protected with arcane devices and traps. Whether you choose to embrace this truth, you owe it to the people who have signed up to work for you to not visit upon them the traumas of your past because that is the only way you think you can perform on the page.

Facing this may be the hardest and most painful truth for any writer. We cling to our delusions, depressions, and darknesses. We mistakenly believe that our creativity is a karmic recompense for the torturous havoc our inner gloom wreaks upon us, and that we must therefore preserve that gloom at all costs lest the creativity follow it on the way out.

Of course, nothing could be further from the truth: while one certainly informs the other, your darkness and your writing come from different places... losing the former - or at least dispelling it long enough to be a human being to your employees - will not affect the latter.

And, if you don't have the time or energy to lay down your affectations once and for all, you can at least cultivate the requisite human decency to shield others from your insanity by building a scaffold of professionalism around yourself. Suffer for your art if you must, but make the effort to prevent others from becoming participants in your daily reenactment of your trauma. If you make a habit of practicing any number of these Laws, even in the most desultory manner, I promise that it will make your life, and your relationships - both in and out of the job - at least a little bit better.

Of course, you don't have to take my word for this.

The final, flithiest little secret of this essay is that

you don't actually have to take my word for anything. That's right, Sparky - in case you didn't notice the *leitmotif* running through the massive spew of verbiage you have so courageously navigated, let me lay it out in pornographic detail...

Every horror story I have told... every tale of madness, rage, and abuse... every last little malfeasant example of selfish and wrongheaded management... was perpetrated by a showrunner "whose work I guarantee you respect and admire."

So there you go. The path is clear for you to be the monster you always knew you could be. Your success - as weighed by critical praise, awards wins, and financial recompense - will have little to do with whether you follow these Eleven Laws.

These may, in fact, be the only Laws you ever see that are not only completely optional, but - in all honesty - tangential to the most commonly accepted definition of success in your chosen field.

So I will just leave them here - as they say in the business of show - "For Your Consideration."

What happens next is up to you.

Me? I'm going to go check my email to see how many of my former bosses have written me angry missives demanding to know why I would nickname them "Sparky."

Notes. There's just no getting away from them.

A LATINO WRITER CALLS B.S. ON HOLLYWOOD'S DIVERSITY EXCUSES

Originally Published in The Hollywood Reporter, August 15, 2018

B eing Latinx in Trump's America is an increasingly precarious business. Even those of us in relative safety and privilege understand that the persistent chorus of "you are less-than" from the President and his mouthpieces is an insult added to injuries ranging from the forced separation and internment of families to the ongoing democide-by-neglect in hurricane-ravaged Puerto Rico. So when the showrunner of the upcoming Latino-led *Magnum P.I.* reboot answered a question about whether his staff includes Latinx writers by asserting it didn't because, "When you're staffing the show, it's incredibly hard to find writers," and added, "We have a very diverse writers room, it just so happens that we don't have any (Latinxs)," I just wanted to chalk it up as business as usual in 'murica and get on with my work.

The next day, however, when the showrunner suddenly remembered having a Latina writer in his staff and tweeted that he had made a "mistake," I was left to wonder: To what mistake exactly was he admitting? Relegating a key creative hire to an afterthought or peddling the demonstrably false excuse that "writers" with the skill to truly articulate the subtlety and nuance of the adventures of Thomas Magnum are really — no, really —

hard to find?

I neither know nor have worked for this showrunner. This is not a demand for investigation or sanction. All he really did — regardless of what he meant — was express a still shockingly common opinion among many showrunners: "Inclusion" is a nuisance, minority writers are a burden to hire and promote, and experienced minority writers are nigh-impossible to find.

I have, by now, heard every crypto-racist, misogynist, ableist, and homophobic showrunner excuse to avoid bringing those who do not resemble them into their writers rooms. These include the perennial ("I can't find anyone who can write my show"), the semi-credible ("I don't have the budget"), the "political" ("I owe that job to my assistant/son/girlfriend/as a favor") and the self-serving ("My show is so unique that I can only hire truly experienced writers"). Once, I even heard a showrunner refuse to hire a gay writer because he only wanted "solid citizens." These excuses continue to flourish and amount to a persistent buzz reinforcing a depressingly pervasive message: Minorities need not apply.

To this fetid panoply of bullshit, our age of both earnest attempts at, and frequent lip service to, inclusion has added a gaggle of victim-blaming showrunner shibboleths like "the studio/network is making me hire minorities," "I can't promote last season's diversity hire because he/she will then cost me money I need on the screen" and the egregious (yet actually said by a showrunner) "we won't be picking up your option because we need 'fresh' diversity."

In spite of the occasional shaming of those who slip up in public, there is little incentive for change. Too many showrunners want to be left alone, be praised for token gestures, and be enabled in the belief that they have earned the right to discriminate by dint of profit, longevity or "genius." By and large, their wishes are granted with impunity.

If you recognize yourself in the above, you have no cause for alarm. If you can avoid saying anything overtly racist at a press tour, your position is probably safe. You do, however, have a choice. You can either do the job of entertaining America with some competence (and by "competence" I mean "realizing that a massive demographic shift is happening and there are greater profits to be made by accurately reflecting the country's makeup in front of and behind the camera") or eventually perish as an evolutionary dead-end. Latinx creators — and every other marginalized group — will find a way to tell their stories (and even those of Ferrari-driving manly-man private investigators) with or without you. The question is: Do you want to participate in the future or pass away into cushy irrelevance with little else to show for it than a few measly seasons of outdated television?

ACKNOWLEDGEMENTS

Lee Thompson did not merely typeset and design this book, he is the reason I have books at all. His talent and unyielding good cheer are far more than I deserve.

Colby Elliott, who produced the audio version of this book and its predecessor has been a source of encouragement, and occasionally, benign pressure, to make this book happen. I'm glad he pushed.

Grant Carmichael deserves recognition for coming out of "retirement" for this project. You honor me, sir!

The Shamers - and they know who they are - are the living platonic ideal of mutual support, inspiration, and friendship.

Without Jose Molina - and our "Children of Tendu" podcast - many of the concepts in these essays would have never found their way to the page. I am honored to be his "replacement Puerto Rican."

I spend a fair bit of time talking about my unique relationship with John Corey in "The Eleven Laws of Showrunning" and don't want him to get too big a head, but he is the front line for pretty much everything I ever have to say.

My mother and father live - day in and out - a life of mentorship and philanthropy. They embody leadership by example, and I aspire to follow in their footsteps.

Above all, Sarah and Indy are the reason I have faith in a future that is wide open, full of promise, and worth seeing.

ABOUT THE AUTHOR

photo by stephen lemieux

In addition to a career spanning over twenty-five years as writer and producer of television, comic books, film, and transmedia content, Javier Grillo-Marxuach is a staunch advocate of mentorship and transparency. He co-hosted and co-created the Children of Tendu podcast (available for free on iTunes, Stitcher, and at childrenoftendu.com) to share his years of experience with aspiring writers and television fans alike.

Grillo-Marxuach's pilot pitches, bibles, and scripts are also available free of charge for educational purposes at his website, www.OKBJGM.com. Grillo-Marxuach also administers the Grillo-Marxuach Family Fellowship for graduate screenwriting students at the University of Southern California, and the Grillo-Marxuach Family Scholarship for undergraduate creative writing students at the Dietrich College of his Alma Mater, Carnegie-Mellon University.

Javier Grillo-Marxuach was born in San Juan, Puerto Rico, and his name is pronounced "HA-VEE-AIR GREE-JOE MARKS-WATCH".

Made in the USA
Middletown, DE
15 February 2019